THE
CROSS
OF
CHRIST

THE
CROSS
OF
CHRIST

JAMES H. TODD

MOODY PRESS
CHICAGO

© 1935, 2001 by
MOODY BIBLE INSTITUTE

All Scripture quotations, unless otherwise indicated, are taken from the
New King James Version. Copyright © 1979, 1980, 1982 by Thomas Nelson,
Inc. Used by permission. All rights reserved.

Scripture quotations marked KJV are taken from the King James Version.

Library of Congress Cataloging-in-Publication Data

Todd, James Henry, 1864–
    The cross of Christ / by James Todd.— [Rev. ed.].
        p. cm.
    ISBN 0-8024-5216-7
    1. Atonement. I. Title

BT265.3 .T63 2001
232'.3—dc21

2001030858

1 3 5 7 9 10 8 6 4 2

CONTENTS

NOTE TO OUR READERS

The ultimate impact of any book can be measured by how well the author communicates on a particular subject. The accuracy of the message and its relevance to the reader are also critical elements that distinguish a select group of books that are available. Most important, those books that build on the foundation of the Bible, with an overriding goal of glorifying God, are the ones that will stand the test of time.

This group of books, taken from the archives of Moody Press, meet those criteria. They are clear in their presentation and easy to read and apply to your life. At the same time, they do not compromise on substance, while presenting strong arguments that remain relevant to today's reader.

The authors write with elegance and conviction; their passion will inspire you. We have chosen to use the New King James Version of the Bible, which maintains the beauty and grace of the original King James Version while being highly readable in today's language.

This series of books is part of our Life Essentials™ line of products because the books fit so well with the Life Essentials' objective: to help the readers stay focused on the essentials of life by keeping God at the center of all they do, grounding them in those truths that build their faith and obedience to the triune God.

We pray that these books will bless and help you in your walk of faith, just as they have done for followers of Jesus Christ in past generations.

THE PUBLISHER

CHAPTER ONE

THE DEATH OF CHRIST

"CHRIST DIED." THESE ARE MOMENTOUS words that form one of the most remarkable statements to be found in the Scriptures.

Death means sin, for "the soul who sins shall die," and the "wages of sin is death." "Through one man sin entered into the world, and death through sin" (Ezekiel 18:20; Romans 6:23; 5:12). The fact of universal death is the great proof of the awful fall of the first man through his yielding to the temptation of the serpent. But those words, "Christ died," tell us of the death of One who was sinless, for Christ never sinned in thought or word or deed.

Not only was it true that He never did anything wrong,

but throughout His whole life everything He did was right and good and perfect. He lived an absolutely perfect life and could say of His relationship with the Father, "I always do those things that please Him" (John 8:29). At the close of His life, He was able to say, too, "I have glorified You on the earth." In every thought and word and act, He perfectly did the will of God and was always pleasing to Him, the very delight of His heart. And yet He died. He tasted death for everyone (see Hebrews 2:9).

There is nothing really beautiful in death; it is an enemy. It is opposed to God, for He is life indeed. Death means separation from God, and it separates friends in this world. The very day that Adam sinned, separation from God took place, for his communion with God was broken. Instead of confidence in God and close communion with Him, fear and doubt came in, and Adam tried to hide from God.

All sin separates the sinner from God, and if sin is not put away, it will separate him from the face of God forever. But just as He sought out Adam so that he might be restored to fellowship and sent the Lord Jesus Christ into the world that He might die for the sinner, God has shown that it is not His will that anyone should be separated from Him eternally. By His death on the cross Christ put away sin and made it possible for everyone, however sinful, to come to God and be received into the most blessed fellowship. All who do come will be with Him eternally, dwelling in His holy presence without any possibility of ever being cast out.

THE NECESSARY DEATH OF CHRIST

It was an absolute necessity for Christ to die. He came for that very purpose. He announced to His disciples again and again that He would be delivered into the hands of wicked men and be killed. He was the "Lamb slain from the foundation of the world" (Revelation 13:8). And even before the foundation of the world He was foreordained by God to be the Lamb by whose precious blood believers were to be redeemed. The death of Christ on the cross was the very center of God's great plan of redemption, and upon it depends every blessing purposed by God.

Christ did not come to set before men and women a beautiful example of a life of love and goodness, so that by following it they might attain to heaven. Nor did He come to teach people a perfect system of ethics for them to practice and so make their lives good and acceptable to God. Nor was it to work miracles—healing and helping the sick and poor and sorrowful, showing that He was God. No, He came to die. He "did not come to be served, but to serve, and to give His life a ransom for many" (Matthew 20:28). He certainly came to set up a wonderful kingdom on the earth, bringing righteousness and peace to the whole world, but that could only come by way of the Cross; for there can be no righteousness or peace or blessing in any manner, unless sin is put away; and the only answer to sin is death.

THE VOLUNTARY DEATH OF CHRIST

"Christ died." His death was voluntary. He gave Himself an offering to God. No one, not even Satan himself, could take His life from Him. Death could not touch Him. He was deathless, for He was sinless. He boldly declared, "I lay down My life that I may take it again. No one takes it from Me, but I lay it down of Myself. I have power to lay it down, and I have power to take it again" (John 10:17–18).

The great fact that it was His own act in giving up His life is wonderfully borne out by each of the evangelists in their records. Matthew says He "yielded up His spirit" (27:50). Mark and Luke use the same phrase, He "breathed His last" (Mark 15:37, 39; Luke 23:46), meaning He breathed out His spirit, a phrase never used of men. John's statement is, "He gave up His spirit" (19:30).

Each one pointed to His death as being a deliberate act and not merely the result of weakness or exhaustion; nor was it of men. It must have been voluntary, for if forced it would arouse a protest that would be justified. It was a witness to His deity, for the centurion looking on was convinced that He was none other than the Son of God.

The law demands death as the penalty for sin, and the sinner must die unless someone voluntarily takes his place, and that substitute must be an innocent one. Jesus Christ, the Lamb of God, impelled by love transcendent, voluntarily died. And God so loved the world that He voluntarily gave Him up to the death of the cross; He did not spare Him one awful blow of the extreme penalty due to sin. The full acceptance by God of that willing sacrifice was signified by His raising Christ from among the dead. And now it remains for sinners to voluntarily accept Him as their substitute, and by so doing receive the full and free forgiveness of all their sins and find perfect acceptance with God in Christ. As surely as the sacrifice was voluntary, so surely must the faith that accepts its benefits be voluntary. Force in either case would be unrighteous.

THE DEATH OF CHRIST CERTAIN

The death of Christ was certified, for before Pilate would give up the body he made sure that Jesus was dead. The soldiers who broke the legs of the thieves in order to be sure that they were dead, refrained from such an act in the case of Christ, for He was already dead. Little did they realize how accurately they were fulfilling the Word of God, which had foretold that not a bone of Him would be broken (see Psalm 34:20). Then He was buried, and it is the dead who are buried. His burial is a witness to the fact of His death.

To question or deny the death of Christ is to give the lie to God and to deny passage after passage of the Word of God. If He did not die, as some dare to state, then He was a liar, for He said He would. The Word of God is broken, there is no salvation, and men are utterly hopeless.

In six different places in the New Testament, the words "gave Himself" occur, bringing out further this blessed fact that He died voluntarily, and that on behalf of others. Three passages teach that His death was voluntary, that it was vicarious, and that it was expiatory:

"Who gave Himself for our sins, that He might deliver us from this present evil age, according to the will of our God and Father" (Galatians 1:4).

"Who gave Himself a ransom for all" (1 Timothy 2:6).

"Who gave Himself for us, that He might redeem us from every lawless deed and purify for Himself His own special people, zealous for good works" (Titus 2:14).

Those three passages indicate clearly that all relationships with God and Christ are determined by the Cross of Christ. Deliverance from sins, from every lawless act, and from the world itself is procured by the voluntary payment of the ransom required. The word "gave" in these verses has the sense of a gift, and that a *free* one.

The other three passages are in Galatians and Ephesians:

"The Son of God, who loved me and gave Himself for me" (Galatians 2:20).

"Christ also has loved us and given Himself for us" (Ephesians 5:2).

"Christ also loved the church and gave Himself for her" (Ephesians 5:25).

The word "gave" in these verses means delivered over into the hands of another. He delivered Himself over to death. The giving of Himself was the expression of His love, and it was personal: "for me," "for us," and "for [the church]." Each of these passages in the order given is connected with faith, love, and hope. And like the previous three passages, they emphasize the death of Christ as being voluntary and vicarious.

CHAPTER TWO

THE CRUCIFIXION
OF CHRIST

NOT ONLY IS THE FACT of the death of Christ of the greatest importance, but the manner of that death must ever be borne in mind in order to appreciate its true value.

"We preach Christ crucified" was the assertion of the apostle Paul to the Corinthians, that being the very first truth he emphasized when he came amongst them with the Gospel (1 Corinthians 1:23). The humbling of Christ, and His coming down to take the form of a servant, being made in the likeness of men, found its climax in His death on the cross (Philippians 2:6–8).

Death by crucifixion was both cruel and shameful; it was the punishment meted out to criminals, and that of the worst kind. It meant excruciating suffering, often of a prolonged nature, going on not only for hours but at times for days. It was not a form of punishment carried out by the Jews, for their law did not allow that. For that reason Jesus was handed over to the Romans, and His crucifixion by them was demanded by the Jewish leaders. "He was numbered with the transgressors," for He was crucified between two thieves. Even they railed on Him, though later one repented and appealed to the Lord Jesus to remember him in His kingdom. In response, he was given the assurance by Christ that on that very day he would be in paradise with Him.

The cross, too, upon which Christ was nailed was evidently the one which had been prepared for Barabbas, the robber and murderer, so it was indeed upon a malefactor's cross that He suffered. And that very fact sets forth most graphically the truth of substitution at the very time of His suffering, for He, the innocent one, was put on the cross of the rebel who was set free. And not only did the cross mean suffering, but the victim was stripped and exposed shamefully to the gaze and contempt of the rabble crowd surrounding the cross. It was a place of most awful ignominy and disgrace.

And then it meant a curse, and that the curse of God; for according to the law of God "cursed is everyone who hangs on a tree" (Galatians 3:13). So that the One to whom all blessing truly belonged, and through whom all blessing comes, was put in the place of the curse; but it was thus that the blessing of God might be assured to all who believe on Him (see Galatians 3:13–14).

THE SUFFERINGS OF CHRIST

The intensity of the sufferings endured by Christ on the cross is borne witness to by the cries which came from His lips: "My God, My God, why have You forsaken Me?" (Matthew 27:46); and then shortly before He expired, "I thirst." The former indicates what the cross meant to Him as the sin-bearer, when it brought about separation from God even for a moment. For there He was made sin, and God cannot look upon sin, which He hates. And hence it was that He spared not His own Son. The cry of thirst would signify something of the intense physical pain He was enduring, relieved somewhat by the vinegar given to Him.

But there may be some danger in dwelling upon the physical aspect of His sufferings and in losing sight of what they meant mentally and otherwise. He could not but shrink with revulsion from sin and its penalty, for He was sinless and loved righteousness and holiness.

What the suffering, shame, and agony of the cross meant to God the Father should also be taken into consideration, for surely it was an awful sight to Him to behold His well-beloved Son, the darling of His heart, in that awful place of guilt and judgment. And yet we know that "God was in Christ reconciling the world to Himself" (2 Corinthians 5:19). It was God who delivered Him up to the cross for us. What a manifestation of love to sinners! What wisdom in providing such a ransom for guilty rebels! What power in giving Him over to death—even the death of the cross!

A study of the instances where the words *cross* and *crucify* occur is enlightening. Linking together the different statements in the Gospels and counting as one those that correspond, one will find the word *cross* in just seven places. Three of these are in the Synoptic Gospels, and four in the gospel of John. In the Epistles the term is used fully eleven times. The word *crucify* occurs much more frequently in both the Gospels and the Epistles. On the way to the place of the crucifixion, the cross was laid on Simon to carry for Jesus. The Synoptic Gospels state that Simon bore the cross, but John says Jesus bore it. The cry from those standing around the cross was for Him to come down from it, if He were the Son of God; and then later the chief priests and scribes and elders took up the same cry, taunting Him with being the King of Israel. The title written by Pilate was put on the cross. Mention is made of those who were standing by the cross when Christ addressed His mother and John, and then there is the statement that the bodies were not allowed to remain on the cross all night.

The word *crucified* occurs thirty times in the Gospels and invariably is connected with the action of Pilate in delivering Christ up to be put to death by the soldiers, and with the demands made by the chief priests and rulers to have Him crucified. Calvary, or Golgotha, the place where He was crucified, also receives mention, for the very place had its significance. Golgotha is the New Testament rendering of Gilgal, on the borders of the land of Canaan, where the reproach of Egypt was rolled away (Joshua 5:2–9). That was the place from whence the Israelites went forth on their march of conquest in the land and to which they returned again and again after different victories. Even so, it is to Golgotha, or Calvary, that the believer turns, for there he sees his reproach rolled away; and from that place he goes forth again and again to victory and the conquest of his enemies. And it is to the Cross he must turn constantly for renewed strength, courage, and comfort, as he faces life with its conflicts.

On the day of Pentecost, the apostle Peter charged those to whom he was speaking with having crucified and slain Christ by the hands of wicked men; and later, when brought before the Council, together with other disciples, he charged them with having crucified this Jesus whom God raised from the dead. It is in the epistles to the Corinthians and the Galatians that the word *crucified* is found nine times, and it occurs once in Hebrews and once in Revelation. In Corinthians the apostle testified that he had gone to Corinth preaching "Christ crucified" and that he had "determined not to know anything among [them] except Jesus Christ, and Him crucified" (1 Corinthians 1:23; 2:2). He asserted that had the rulers known who Jesus truly was "they would not have crucified the Lord of glory" (1 Corinthians 2:8). Christ crucified had been set forth before the Galatians publicly, so that they knew the truth of the Cross and its meaning; therefore their departure from the truth of the Gospel was inexcusable. Three times in the epistle to the Galatians is the word *crucified* connected with the position of the believer as identified with Christ in His death (Galatians 2:20; 5:24; 6:14).

OPPOSITION TO THE CROSS

The Cross is mentioned in six of the Epistles, and in every one it is opposed in some particular way. In 1 Corinthians it is the theme of the preaching of the apostle, and while it is a message of salvation to believers and meant the very power of God to them, it is only foolishness to those who are perishing. The Jews were seeking a sign and the Greeks wisdom. The sign represents ritualism, and wisdom stands for rationalism—the two great opponents of the Cross right down through the ages.

The natural heart is always looking for something outwardly beautiful, something that will appeal to the senses; or it is demanding some explanation or reason before accepting the truth and acting in simple faith.

But the Cross of Christ does not appeal to the emotions in that way, nor is its meaning and power known by the intellect alone; but where faith grasps its significance, it becomes to the believer the wisdom and the power of God, saving and blessing.

There are three references to the Cross in Galatians that show its truth and power, and that the opposition on the part of man comes from the flesh seeking to obtain blessing by some work; thus refusing to recognize the completeness of the work of the Cross and the fullness of the salvation provided thereby. It is therefore a stumbling block and an offense to mankind naturally, for it takes from men and women all glory or credit in salvation, which is by faith alone.

It is the work of Christ for the sinner that counts, and then the work of the Spirit in him, perfecting that which is begun by receiving Christ. The enmity in the heart of the Jew towards those of other nations is contrary to the Cross, which puts all people in the position of guilty sinners. It was at the cross that that enmity was slain, so that all who believe on Christ are brought into oneness in Christ; that is the testimony of Ephesians.

Philippians is an epistle of experience where doctrine is not given prominence. There self-indulgence, or the pampering of the flesh, which evidences pride and self-conceit, is shown to be in opposition to the life set forth as worthy of those who seek to follow Christ; for Jesus humbled Himself and submitted to the death of the cross, and by that condescension and self-sacrifice showed what true devotion to God meant.

Colossians was written to refute the errors taught by the gnostics, who held matter to be evil—gnostics who also took from Christ His absolute deity as Creator and as Head of the old and new creations. The expression "the blood of His cross" is therefore peculiar to that letter, for by it peace was made and the sinner reconciled to God. The Cross broke down the enmity in the minds of men, shown by wicked works, bringing believers to a place of friendship with God. Then in chapter two, where the position of the believer in Christ is shown to be perfect and settled, the complete answer to the law is given in two statements regarding the power of the Cross. By it Christ blotted out "the handwriting of ordinances . . . against us, . . . nailing it to his cross" (Colossians 2:14 KJV). The "blotting out" refers to the custom of erasing or rubbing out from wax tablets any accusation or charge against a person; for when a debt was settled and paid, the part held by the creditor and that in the hands of the debtor were nailed to the door of his house as a witness that it was canceled. The law was therefore met and completely answered at the cross. The Cross has brought to the believer the very fullness of blessing, while any law keeping or legality would only rob him of such.

In Hebrews 12:2, Jesus is set forth as "the author and finisher of our faith," and His endurance of the cross with its shame in view of the "joy . . . set before

Him" is an example to all who are of faith. That is the great incentive to them to press forward in the race and to be prepared to accept chastening at the hand of God, which is the portion of all who become the sons of God. It is unbelief that causes men and women to turn from the Cross and refuse to accept the discipline that comes from the Lord so that His children "may be partakers of His holiness" (12:10).

THE CROSS IN THE PSALMS

Two psalms stand out in particular as setting forth the experiences through which the Lord Jesus passed in His sufferings on the cross. One is Psalm 22, which has been called the psalm of the sob. The first half of it describes how intensely the Lord suffered when giving Himself up to death. He was not only forsaken by God but mocked and taunted by His enemies and left alone by those who were His followers.

The other is Psalm 69, where the prominent thought throughout is that of reproach; for it is the trespass offering that is presented, and it was an offering which showed sin to be wrong and injurious. Reproach and shame are the ideas stressed, and these are connected with sin.

On the cross Christ was forsaken by God for a short time that we might never be shut out of His presence, even for a moment. He took the place of reproach and shame so that every divine blessing and God's continual favor might be the eternal portion of those who come to Him.

CHAPTER THREE

THE FINISHED WORK
OF CHRIST

THE CRY OF JESUS ON THE CROSS just before yielding up His spirit, "It is finished!" (John 19:30), was one of His great utterances and full of significance. It was just one word, "finished" or "done." The Greek word is rendered in other passages by the English words *make an end, accomplish, fulfill, perform, fill up, pay,* and *go over.* The word therefore has the meaning of completeness, fullness, or filling up.

By the sacrificial death of Christ on the cross, a complete salvation was provided for everyone who will accept it by faith. The death of Christ, which made atonement for sin, was therefore the one and only way of salvation provided by God for all sinners. The cry of Christ, "It is finished!" was a triumphant one, announcing a work completely accomplished on behalf of a sinful world; and on the ground of that finished work, and it alone, every sinner may find perfect and eternal acceptance with God.

The words "accomplished" and "might be fulfilled" in John 19:28 are from the same Greek word as "finished" in verse 30. At the cross, the word of God regarding the need of a perfect sacrifice to atone for sin and thus put it away found fulfillment in the death of Christ. Every sacrifice recorded in the Old Testament from that of Abel down had in view the one great atoning sacrifice of Christ at Calvary as the Lamb of God, taking away the sin of the world. All bore witness to the absolute necessity of the death of a spotless victim before there could be any approach to God whatever.

God's Word is the expression of His will or His purpose, and in offering up Himself on the cross, Christ fulfilled the will of God. This is realized by those who come to the Cross as penitent sinners and there enter into its meaning and significance, both in its Godward and manward aspects. There all doubts and fears are dispelled, and faith finds a place of rest. That was the experience of the doubting Thomas, for it was when he saw the marks of the nails in the hands of Christ and the wound made by the spear in His side that he believed and rested. The Cross is the pledge, or guarantee, by God of the fulfillment of all of His great and most precious promises. The Cross is also the assurance that He brought about all His purposes of blessing for His people and for the whole world.

THE LOVE OF GOD MANIFESTED

"By this we know love, because He laid down His life for us" (1 John 3:16). "In this the love of God was manifested toward us, that God has sent His only begotten Son into the world, that we might live through Him. In this is love, not that we loved God, but that He loved us and sent His Son to be the propitiation for our sins" (1 John 4:9–10). The Cross of Christ was the one great manifestation of the love of God, for there the very fullness of that love was shown forth in the Father's giving of His only Son as a sacrifice for sinners. "He . . . did not spare His own Son, but delivered Him up for us all" (Romans 8:32), and that to a shameful death for His enemies, who deserved only judgment at His hand.

The Cross witnesses to divine love in all its fullness, revealing a holy God to whom sin is hateful and an abomination but who gave His well-beloved Son, the very darling of His heart, in order that sin might be put away and sinners brought into fellowship with Him.

Nor did God spare His Son from all that sin deserved through the breaking of His holy law, thus bringing upon sinners the curse of the law and the wrath of God. He so loved the world that He gave His Son unstintingly and unreservedly to death, even pouring upon His blessed head the vials of His wrath, so that He might offer to sinners a full and free salvation as His free gift of love. "Greater love has no one than this, than to lay down one's life for his friends" (John 15:13); but at the cross God gave His only Son as a sacrifice for His enemies. Christ "suffered once for sins, the just for the unjust" (1 Peter 3:18).

SIN REVEALED AT THE CROSS

It was at the cross that sin found its full expression and showed itself in all its heinousness. All classes of men united at the cross to crucify the Son of God. Their actions were a full manifestation of sin, exposing the utter depravity of the human heart and its revolt against all that is pure and holy and true. There sin showed itself in taking that One who was perfectly pure and holy, ever meek and lowly, never injuring a creature, and nailing Him to a malefactor's cross as an object of shame and ignominy. Could there be any act more diabolical, or anything more fiendish? There sin surely gave vent to itself in all its fullness and showed what an awful monster it is when unchecked and unrestrained.

It was not the riffraff and the rabble that so acted but the very highest in the land and those who were the religious leaders of the people. For the natural heart of man, even though religious and outwardly respectable and honest, is capable of the vilest and most heinous sin. At the cross sin showed itself in its envy, hatred, and malice towards the Son of God and in the scoffing, mocking, and jeering railed at Him when He was suffering the most intense agony. That surely was sin in all its fullness.

SIN PUT AWAY AT THE CROSS

And there at the cross of Christ all sin and every sin were met and answered fully and forever. "The Lord has laid on Him the iniquity of us all" (Isaiah 53:6). "He made Him . . . to be sin" (2 Corinthians 5:21). There God searched out all that sin was and all that it deserved and met all on the head of His own Son.

The Cross of Christ is the full and final answer to all that sin is and to all the judgment that sin deserves. At the cross sin was abolished, for "He has appeared to put away sin by the sacrifice of Himself" (Hebrews 9:26). The sacrifice of the Lord Jesus Christ on the cross is a full and complete remedy for all sin. The whole question of sin as guilt, demanding the judgment of God, was there dealt with, and that means that every sinner coming to the Cross and by faith beholding Christ as a personal Savior, is fully absolved from all sin and freed completely from all judgment because of it, and that eternally. The salvation procured at the Cross is full, free, eternal, and complete from the moment that it is received by faith.

JUDGMENT SATISFIED AT THE CROSS

"For in the hand of the Lord there is a cup, and the wine is red; it is fully mixed, and He pours it out" (Psalm 75:8). At the cross Christ drank of that cup and drained it to the very dregs, for there the awful judgment of God for sin fell upon Him. God's wrath lay "heavy upon me, and You have afflicted me with all Your waves" (Psalm 88:7; see also Psalm 42:7). There "the Lord has laid on Him the iniquity of us all" (Isaiah 53:6). The words "laid on" mean "caused to meet upon." God's fiat from the beginning was "In the day that you eat of it you shall surely die" (Genesis 2:17). Sin brings death, and that means separation from God—that is its judgment.

The judgment for sin, and that to its utmost, was passed over then and afterwards met by Christ, so that God now assures us that "there is therefore now no condemnation to those who are in Christ Jesus" (Romans 8:1). Everyone believing on Christ crucified and raised again is justified and cleared fully and finally from all the guilt and condemnation of sin. The believer is not only pardoned and cleared from all judgment, but he is declared righteous "in Christ," having the righteousness of God.

"Finished," "complete," full" are the words that come down to us from the Cross, telling so wondrously the fullness of the love of God, the awfulness and heinousness of sin, and exhibiting God's judgment upon it. They also reveal to us the perfect salvation provided for every sinner who will but accept it as the free gift of God and that by simple faith. The Cross makes it possible for God to save freely and fully every sinner who comes there by faith; but it also makes it impossible for God to save anyone, however good, any other way.

Oh, that the cry coming from the very lips of the Lord Jesus Himself, and ringing down through the ages, would come home to everyone hearing it, so that the full significance of "It is finished!" might be realized.

CHAPTER FOUR

THE CRISIS OF
THE CROSS

THE FIRST TWELVE CHAPTERS of John's gospel present the public ministry of Christ. From the thirteenth chapter onward He is seen in private with His disciples, until we come to John 18, where history is resumed. He is the Light of the World shining out in its darkness, and in these first twelve chapters the light and the darkness are in conflict, for there is a gradual development of belief and unbelief.

John 12 is the culmination, for judgment is announced in verse 31, where are recorded the words of Christ "Now is the judgment of this world; now the ruler of this world will be cast out."

The Greek word for "judgment" is *krisis*, hence our English word *crisis*. *Judgment, damnation, condemnation* are the chief renderings of the word, and its meaning is given as "separation"; for judgment means separating the good from the bad. Christ was pointing to the Cross looming before Him as the crisis, for that was the great crisis of the world. It was the great crisis in His own life, and it was the one great event to which He ever looked forward during His life on earth.

The Cross was before Him from the moment of His coming into the world right on until He laid down His life there as a voluntary sacrifice. In fact, it had been before Him previous to His coming into the world, for it was determined by God in the eternal ages. He was foreordained to be the Lamb of God and that before the foundation of the world. It was the divine plan, the eternal purpose, that Christ should come into the world and give His life a ransom for all men (see 1 Timothy 2:6).

THE WORLD'S CRISIS

The Cross was the crisis of this world, the pivotal center of all God's dealings with it. It is not only the central point in the purpose of God for the world, but it is the only determining factor in the history of the world and in the destiny of mankind. By virtue of the Cross and through its work, "the kingdoms of this world [will yet] become the kingdoms of our Lord and of His Christ" (Revelation 11:15). The Cross makes it possible for God to reach out to the utmost limits of the world and offer salvation to all, apart from any racial position, personal privilege, or individual merit.

At the cross the world took sides against God in rejecting the Son of God, and thereby forfeited any claim it could possibly have had upon Him. There the world manifested its guilt and condemnation of God, for all mankind was represented by those who surrounded that wooden cross, mocking and jeering at the blessed Son of God.

"For God so loved the world that He gave His only begotten Son" (John 3:16), and in giving Him to the awful death of the cross, God the Father placed upon the Son the whole responsibility of salvation. That means that everyone is shut up absolutely to faith in Christ and to faith alone for salvation.

THE CRISIS OF SATAN

The Cross was a crisis for Satan, for there he was destroyed or "brought to naught," as were also his works. Just when the devil was putting forth all his malice and hatred against the Son of God, and thinking that he was triumphing over Him, he was being most truly defeated.

Christ took part of flesh and blood that He might destroy him who had the power of death, that is, the devil. That destruction was his annulling, robbing Satan of final power and authority; and it meant his final doom of being cast into the lake of fire. "The Son of God was manifested, that He might destroy the works

37

of the devil" (1 John 3:8). There the word "destroy" means to loose or unloose as of bonds, illustrated in the case of the woman in Luke 13, bound by Satan for eighteen years.

The prince of this world, who is the prince of the power of the air, will yet be cast out of that sphere into the world for a short time, before being bound for the thousand years, but will eventually be cast into the lake of fire, to be there eternally. What a crisis the Cross was indeed for that enemy of God and man. And thank God, every sinner who comes to the Cross in simple faith may be delivered from the wiles and devices and power of his adversary, Satan; for God "delivered us [believers] from the power of darkness and conveyed us into the kingdom of the Son of His love" (Colossians 1:13).

THE CRISIS OF EVERY MAN AND WOMAN

The greatest crisis that ever comes to any man or woman is the Cross. It means either life or death to everyone. To the sinner convinced of his sin, turning to the Cross of Christ and believing on Him as a personal Savior, it means eternal life and eternal salvation; but to those who turn away from the Cross in unbelief and pride, it means eternal death or separation from God forever and ever. The Cross is therefore a crisis for everyone.

For the believer in Christ it is surely a crisis, for there his sin was judged by God and by the sacrifice of

Christ put away forever. There he is crucified to the world and the world to him. There the law of God, which cursed and condemned him, was completely satisfied on his behalf, and now he is dead to the law (see Romans 7:4–6). There he himself was crucified with Christ, thereby delivered from all his old life and shut up in Christ to a new life of blessing and liberty. "Those who are Christ's have crucified the flesh with its passions and desires" (Galatians 5:24).

The Cross takes the believer out from under sin and its condemnation into a place of forgiveness and acceptance. By it he is cleared from all guilt and made righteous in Christ. His destiny is changed from one of eternal death and woe into one of eternal bliss. And all this is made sure by the Cross and by the Cross alone—and that the moment he believes on Christ as a personal Savior.

Everything in creation was brought into being on account of the Cross of Christ. It was God's great objective in His work of creation, and His eternal purpose made in a past eternity. In a coming eternity, it will be the one great event never to be forgotten. It shall ever be looked back to as the one determining event in time, settling the destiny of all things for all time.

By virtue of the Cross, the Lamb will sit upon the throne of glory, surrounded by the vast host of the redeemed, whose hearts and voices will be united in ascribing all praise and honor and glory to Him who loved them and loosed them from their sins by His blood. Their song will be: "You are worthy to take the scroll, and to open its seals; for You were slain, and have redeemed us to God by Your blood out of every tribe and tongue and people and nation, and have made us kings and priests to our God; and we shall reign on the earth" (Revelation 5:9–10).

CHAPTER FIVE

THE VICARIOUS DEATH OF CHRIST

"CHRIST DIED FOR THE UNGODLY." "Christ died for us." "Christ died for our sins." Christ "died for all" (Romans 5:8; 1 Corinthians 15:3; 2 Corinthians 5:14). These statements show that He did not die for Himself; nor was it for any cause in Himself that He died, but on behalf of others. There was absolutely nothing in Him demanding death or making it at all possible for death to touch Him. For death means sin, and He "did no sin"; He "knew no sin"; and "in him is no sin" (1 Peter 2:22; 2 Corinthians 5:2; 1 John 3:5 KJV).

Christ was ever perfectly sinless, never in any way being tainted by sin or having even the suspicion of it. He was holy, harmless, undefiled, and separate from sinners.

Some have argued that Christ died for the elect or for the church, but it is said distinctly that He "gave Himself a ransom for all"; and again, "He Himself is the propitiation . . . for the whole world" (1 Timothy 2:6; 1 John 2:2). Remember, "He died *for all*" (italics added). His death came on behalf of all people, even though many may not believe it or accept His death as for them.

He said, "I, if I am lifted up from the earth, will draw all peoples to Myself" (John 12:32). The "all" does not mean all without exception but all without distinction. For in His day the Jews did not believe in any salvation outside of the Jewish pale, and if Gentiles were to be blessed, it was only as they were prepared to come into the Jewish fold as proselytes. Christ did not mean that His death would bring universal salvation, but that it would provide salvation available for all who would accept it by faith. The proclamation of His forerunner, John the Baptist, was: "Behold! The Lamb of God who takes away the sin of the world!" (John 1:29); and from the lips of the Lord Himself fell these notable words, "For God so loved the world that He gave His only begotten Son, that whoever believes in Him should not perish but have everlasting life" (John 3:16).

There are fourteen passages where the death of Christ is stated as being vicarious, six of those being in the gospel of John. In three of them we have His own words, saying that He would give His life "for the life of the world" (6:51); that "the good shepherd gives His life for the sheep" (10:11); and "I lay down my life for the sheep" (10:15). The other three are in John 11, being the statements of the high priest: "That one man should die for the people, and not that the whole nation should perish. . . . And not for that nation only, but also that He would gather together in one the children of God" (vv. 50–52).

The other eight occurrences are in the Epistles, as follows: "He who did not spare his own Son, but delivered Him up for us all" (Romans 8:32); "He made Him . . . to be sin for us" (2 Corinthians 5:21); He "[became] a curse for us" (Galatians 3:13); "that He, by the grace of God, might taste death for everyone" (Hebrews 2:9); "Christ also suffered for us" (1 Peter 2:21); "Christ also suffered once for sins, the just for the unjust" (1 Peter 3:18); "Christ suffered for us in the flesh" (1 Peter 4:1); and "He laid down His life for us" (1 John 3:16).

In addition to these fourteen passages, there are seven others where the expression "died for" occurs, each one being connected with some particular doctrine relating to the Christian life. There are three in Romans, three in 2 Corinthians, and one in 1 Thessalonians. In between these is the great Gospel statement of 1 Corinthians 15:3, "Christ died for our sins according to the Scriptures." That is the great basal statement of the Gospel, for apart from the atoning death of Christ on the cross there is no Gospel for lost sinners and no salvation to offer them. In Romans 5 we have the two statements "Christ died for the ungodly," and "Christ died for us" (vv. 6, 8). The first eleven verses of that chapter show the permanence the position of justified believers.

THE BELIEVER'S POSITION ASSURED

Those who are justified by faith have peace with God, being made one with Him in Christ, and stand in the grace into which they are brought, rejoicing in the hope of glory. Their position is made sure by God, who justifies them on the ground of Christ's work of redemption, accepted by faith and faith alone. Any experience through which the believer may pass cannot affect that work of Christ, not even tribulation or sin, for those saved by His death are kept by His life.

Because the love of God is shed abroad in the heart, no fear or doubt can destroy their position, and even their weakness is met by the strength of Christ. Being justified by His blood, their salvation from coming wrath is assured. Christ died for the ungodly, for the weak, for His enemies, for the best as well as the worst; *how much more* then will He save eternally those brought into a place of reconciliation and friendship. Both justification and reconciliation are based on the work of Christ and complete for the believer.

In Romans 14:15 the exhortation is "Do not destroy with your food the one for whom Christ died." That chapter deals with matters of conscience and the responsibility of stronger ones toward their weaker brethren. All are accountable to God for their own actions and will have to stand before the judgment seat of Christ and give an account. In matters of conscience there must be liberty, but at the same time care is called for so that in using one's liberty no offense is caused to others who differ in judgment, particularly any who are weaker and possibly less enlightened. It is the sanctified walk and the recognition of Christ as Lord that are the prominent truths here, along with the judgment seat of Christ.

MOTIVE FOR CHRISTIAN SERVICE

In 2 Corinthians 5:15 there are two statements regarding the death of Christ for others: first, in the words "He died for all"; and then, "that those who live should live no longer for themselves, but for Him who died for them and rose again." Second Corinthians deals with ministry, chapter five bringing out the great motives that prompt true service. The judgment seat of Christ, as it will affect the believer, and the terror of the Lord for the unsaved should impel to earnest service; then the constraining love of Christ, as manifested in the giving of Himself for us, should be the incentive to those who live through Him. For through that death believers are a new creation, and the new life in Christ should be spent for Him to whom it is entirely due. The death of Christ gives the ground and motive for devoted ministry, that of reconciliation, committed to us as ambassadors for Christ.

The opening verses of 1 Thessalonians 5 refer to the day of the Lord, its suddenness and destruction, with warnings to believers against sloth or unwatchfulness; for believers are "sons of the day" and not of the night, and they should therefore "watch and be sober" (see vv. 5, 6). They are to be wakeful and not sleeping. In verses 9–10, we read, "Our Lord Jesus Christ . . . died for us, that whether we wake or sleep, we should live together with Him." This follows the statement that "God hath not appointed us to wrath, but to obtain salvation by our Lord Jesus Christ." The word "obtain" means to acquire or take possession of, and points to the realization of salvation in all its fullness at the coming of Christ. The word "sleep" in the previous verses does not mean death but slothfulness, against which believers are warned. Verse 10 shows that when the Lord comes, all believers will be caught up, and not because of faithfulness or earnestness in life.

The death of Christ is therefore connected with the translation of believers at the coming of the Lord in the air, according to the closing verses of 1 Thessalonians 4. The wrath referred to is the day of wrath coming on the earth, and will be introduced immediately after the rapture of the church at the coming of the Lord. This is one of the plainest and clearest answers to those who teach a special rapture for those who are watching, for it teaches unequivocally that all believers will be taken because Christ died for them.

In these different passages, the vicarious death of Christ is connected with the great truths of justification, reconciliation, ministration, consecration, translation, and presentation, having in the center the great Gospel words about the death, burial, and resurrection of Christ (1 Corinthians 15), and therefore touches us in every aspect of the Christian life. It is the ground of our salvation, of our justification, and our perfect security. It is the great incentive to holiness of walk and to earnestness in service, and it assures us of a certain hope of our translation at the coming of the Lord and of our full realization of salvation for the whole man.

CHAPTER SIX

THE CROSS AND REDEMPTION

ONE OF THE SWEETEST WORDS in the Scriptures is the word *redeemed*, for it is so full of wondrous meaning and significance to the believer. *Redemption* is one of the great words connected with the work of Christ on the cross, expressing the blessed deliverance effected there for all who are under the guilt and bondage of sin. It conveys two great truths, one being that of purchase or buying back by the payment of a ransom, and the other, deliverance from bondage by the ransom paid and by the power of God.

In the Old Testament there are four different words rendered by the English word *redeem;* and in the New Testament the truth is expressed in different forms of two Greek words.

One of the Old Testament words occurs as "redeem" only once (Psalm 136:24 KJV), and means to break off or to separate. Another means to buy and so acquire for oneself or possess, and occurs as "redeemed" in Nehemiah 5:8. It is the word "purchased" in Exodus 15:16, and in Psalms 74:2 and 78:54; in Ruth 4:4–5, 8–9 it is the word "buy." In the other two words there is both the idea of purchase and of deliverance, and from one of them we get the noun "redeemer." The redeemer had to be a near kinsman, so as to have the right to buy back that which had been sold, and also authority to avenge or revenge the wronged one. In Numbers 35:12, 19, 21, 24–25, 27, the avenger or revenger is the redeemer.

Exodus has as its theme redemption, recording the deliverance of God's people from the bondage of Egypt, thus bringing them into liberty as the people of God and into a new relationship with Him as a separated people. It is a type, presenting the truth of all redemption. Israel as the people of God were His by purchase, and He repeatedly delighted to speak of them as "My people," even when they were disobedient and wayward. Because He had purchased them to be His own possession, and in doing so had separated them from other nations, He required them to be holy, for that is the basis of the laws of holiness given in Leviticus (20:26). In the payment of the ransom there is no thought of the price being paid to anyone, though the people are spoken of in a number of places as being sold.

In Judges it is said more than once that God sold them on account of their sin and apostasy, and in Isaiah 50:1, where He is said to have sold them, they are charged with having sold themselves. In their servitude recorded in Judges they were certainly sold to the nations to whom they became slaves, but that does not mean that any ransom was paid to these nations. In Egypt they were sold under Pharaoh, but the ransom was not paid to him. Once in the New Testament the sinner is said to be "sold under sin" (Romans 7:14).

The ruin and bondage of Egypt are typical of the bondage of the sinner under sin and the power of Satan, the god of this age. The books of Exodus and Romans have a correspondence, for in each there are three chief parts: in Exodus they are ruin, redemption, and relationship; and in Romans similarly we have man under sin and in ruin, then redemption by the work of Christ, and finally the practical bearing of the truth on life and conduct.

THE REDEMPTION PRICE PAID

In redemption as a purchase, the prominent thought is the price paid. In Psalm 49, the price paid in redemption is contrasted with all the wealth possessed by rich men, showing how utterly inadequate were all the riches they possessed to pay the required ransom. "For the redemption of their souls is costly, and it shall cease forever" (v. 8). And this last clause may be rendered, "It must be let alone forever," that being considered a more correct translation. It was far too costly for man to face, even had he possessed all the wealth that the world could give. Redemption cannot come about by silver or gold or any other wealth, but only by "the precious blood of Christ."

The New Testament words that speak of redemption as "purchase" are those used of men buying in the market, or forum. Twice, believers are reminded that they "are bought at a price" (1 Corinthians 6:20; 7:23), whereas false teachers are said to deny the Lord who bought them (2 Peter 2:1). In the book of Revelation the great company seen about the throne of God is said to have been redeemed, or bought (Revelation 5:9; 14:4). A stronger word is used in Galatians 3:13 and 4:5, where redemption by Christ is from the law and its curse; and it means to buy out from under, or to buy up, which is the better rendering in Ephesians 5:16 and Colossians 4:5.

The price paid for anything determines its value to the purchaser; the greater the cost, the more an owner prizes the article. No greater price could have been paid than that given by God for our redemption, for it was the precious blood of Christ, His only begotten Son. There can be nothing in the world then so precious in His sight as those who have been bought by the payment of that great price, and it is that which makes it so very blessed to be a child of God. "You are not your own . . . you are bought at a price."

Even by creation we are His, for the maker of any-thing has the prior right to its possession. In Psalm 100 we are told that He has made us, and we are His. That is true of all created beings; and as Creator, God claims the right to the worship and obedience of all the works of His hands, for He is worthy of worship and of trust. It is much more precious, however, to be-long to Him by redemption; for the redeemed are brought into a closer relationship, and His love is real-ized in a particular way. As the price indicates the worth, so believers are as precious to God as His own well-beloved Son, being bought by His own precious blood.

By the pouring out of His blood upon the earth, Christ paid the price necessary to buy as His own the whole world. He was the merchant who found trea-sure in a field and bought the whole field for the sake of it (Matthew 13:44). And that evidently means that all men are His by virtue of that price paid. Again in 2 Peter 2:1, evil men are said to deny the Lord who bought them, showing that the price was paid even for some who despise it. Redemption is surely provided for all, and therefore all may realize the wonderful de-liverance from the bondage of sin and the liberty pur-chased for the children of God, if they will but exercise that simple faith in Christ which brings to them experimentally the salvation provided by His blood. The love and delight that the great heart of God finds in His own beloved Son is the very delight and satisfaction found by Him in those redeemed by His precious blood.

DELIVERANCE BY REDEMPTION

Redemption means not only purchase by payment of the ransom required, but it has in view particularly the setting free of those who have been slaves and in bondage. Deliverance is the prominent idea of redemption in both Testaments. All three words for *redeem* in the Old Testament enforce the truth of freedom or deliverance from bondage. The word rendered "redeemed" in Psalm 136:24 (KJV) is "deliver" in Lamentations 5:8 (KJV), and it is generally translated by the terms "break," or "rend, tear in pieces," meaning violent action. When applied to the work of God in redeeming His people, it points to His mighty power in breaking the forces of evil that held them. There, too, His power shone forth in the destruction of their enemies, the Egyptians. In Egypt their redemption was effected by the sprinkling of the blood, which made them safe from the judgment of God, and then the passage at the Red Sea delivered them from the power of Pharaoh and his hosts. These find their fulfillment in the Cross of Christ and His resurrection from the dead. The Hebrew word referred to is *pehrek*.

Another word in the Hebrew is *padah*, nearly always rendered "redeem." It means to set free, or to let go. The idea of payment is prominent, too, for it is the word used of the half shekel paid as redemption money by the people of Israel. In Psalm 49 it is the word "redemption," where the cost of the ransom is so high it is beyond the wealth of man. It is the word "division" in Exodus 8:23 (KJV), and signifies the separation of the Israelites from the Egyptians, when they were preserved from the judgment poured out on the land in the swarm of flies. The separation of Israel in their redemption was from their old manner of life, so that they might be a holy people; and instead of being under Pharaoh and in bondage to him, they were to be the people of God under His rule.

That redemption typified the redemptive work of Christ, for He is our Passover; and it is by the precious blood of Christ that we are redeemed from our old manner of life, in order that we might be holy even as He is holy (1 Peter 1:16, 19). The very purpose of the coming of Christ was to give His life a ransom for many (Matthew 20:28). "Who gave himself for us, that he might redeem us from all iniquity, and purify unto himself a peculiar people, zealous of good works" (Titus 2:14 KJV). And in Hebrews 9:12, it is declared that the redemption procured by His blood is eternal.

The word most commonly used for *redeem* is the Hebrew word *gaal*, from which comes the kinsman-redeemer and avenger. Leviticus 25 is the great chapter on redemption, teaching the liberty and the joy connected with the Year of Jubilee. It is there that instructions are given regarding the redemption of one sold as a slave, and the restoration of an inheritance that had been lost. In the case of a man sold and unable to redeem himself, it was only someone near of kin who could act for him. His being a near kinsman gave him the right to redeem him; and in addition to that, he needed the necessary wealth so as to be able to pay the required price; and then he had to be willing to do the part called for.

This was beautifully exemplified in the case of Boaz, the mighty man of wealth, who redeemed Ruth and in so doing restored to Naomi the inheritance lost by her husband. He is a type of Christ, who in becoming man, also became our kinsman and so established His right to pay the ransom for our redemption.

This is the truth of Hebrews 2, which follows the description of the glory of Christ as the Son of God in chapter one. Christ in becoming man became the Kinsman-Redeemer of men and so had the right to redeem; and as Son of God all the power and wealth were at His disposal in order to meet all that sin demanded. And the one other condition called for, that of willingness, was manifested by Him also, for He laid down His life voluntarily. As He said, "I lay down My life that I may take it again. No one takes it from Me, but I lay it down of Myself. I have power to lay it down, and I have power to take it again" (John 10:17–18). In his gospel, Luke presents Christ as man and redeemer, and this is the first note of joy and praise in the New Testament.

REDEMPTION UNTO HOLINESS

In the New Testament epistles, redemption as deliverance from sin and evil, committing the redeemed to holiness of life and to loving, devoted service, is far more prominent than the idea of purchase. In Romans, it is the ground of justification, whereby the believer is cleared by God from all charge on account of sin and counted righteous by Him with the very righteousness of God. In Ephesians and Colossians, redemption procures for the believer the full forgiveness of all trespasses, meaning all that was entailed by the fall of man and all the consequences flowing from it. In Titus, we are redeemed from all iniquity or lawlessness, that is, all that is contrary to the will of God, and made His peculiar people, or a peculiar treasure to Him, for His own possession—zealous of good works.

The reference to redemption in 1 Peter has in view the taking of the people of Israel out of Egypt, and it means a change in the whole manner of life, as in their case. The change is from a state of slavery under sin to one of a holy people unto God. The book of Revelation shows that the position of the redeemed in glory, with all its privileges and possibilities throughout eternity, is due entirely to redemption by the blood of Christ. Believers will then realize not only freedom from sin's guilt and power, and even its taint, but in their redeemed bodies will be freed from all tendency to sin. They will have full deliverance from all limitations and weaknesses, and so be unable to fail in any way whatever. That will be the complete emancipation from all the effects of the Fall, and the manifestation of the liberty and glory that belongs to the sons of God.

FULL REDEMPTION PROPHESIED

Creation itself will feel the effects of that great redemptive work, for the whole creation will be delivered from the curse resulting from the Fall and be brought into a place of blessing and fruitfulness even greater than that of Eden. The animal creation is to be changed, and the earth itself, instead of bringing forth thorns and briars, will produce fruit and flowers abundantly. Because of the work of Christ, such wonderful pictures as those presented in Isaiah 35 will be fully realized to the glory of God. This will follow the future redemption of Israel, which is primarily the type in Ruth, for that nation will be restored to their inheritance and planted in their land forever, and will realize all that God purposed for them from the beginning of the world.

"Oh, the depth of the riches both of the wisdom and knowledge of God! How unsearchable are His judgments and His ways past finding out! . . . For of Him, and through Him and to Him are all things, to whom be glory forever" (Romans 11:33, 36).

"All Mine are Yours, and Yours are Mine, and I am glorified in them." That seems to be the central thought which prompted the intercession of the Lord Jesus in His great high-priestly prayer in John 17. He pours out His heart to God for His own that they may be kept, that they may be sanctified, that they may be glorified and finally perfected into oneness with Himself. His one great concern is for those who are His. He longs over them and pleads for their perfecting. That alone will give Him satisfaction. They are His. "Having loved his own which were in the world, he loved them unto the end" (John 13:1 KJV). He loved them perfectly, to the uttermost, with a love which cannot be broken, and which He showed by giving Himself for them.

THE REDEEMED OF THE LORD

And what of those who are redeemed? "You are not your own . . . therefore glorify God in your body" (1 Corinthians 6:19–20) "You were bought at a price; do not become slaves of men" (1 Corinthians 7:23). How far is there a true recognition of our being His and allowing Him to possess us for Himself? What rest of heart, what satisfaction, what confidence this truth should bring to the heart of all who are His! How the truth should prompt to zeal in service and to devotion!

The bride in the Song of Solomon says, "My beloved is mine, and I am his," and later, "I am my beloved's, and my beloved is mine"; and then still later, "I am my beloved's, and his desire is toward me" (Song of Solomon 2:16; 6:3; 7:10). And that last clause means that He cleaves to His own and enriches them with every blessing. His own are bought with a price, are precious to Him, and all because of His infinite love. That is one of the great aspects of redemption, whether in the Old Testament or in the New Testament.

The following note by Bishop H. C. G. Moule is very apt: "I have read of a servant of Christ in the past, a man singularly rich in the gift of spiritual influence over individuals, who was asked to disclose something of his secret. His reply, in essence, was that it lay, as far as he knew, in the sense of profound contentment with his blessed Master, in which his soul was kept through grace. Jesus Christ irradiated him within and for Himself. At the very center of his soul's consciousness, he was deeply happy to belong to his King who had saved him, and to be used by that great and holy Possessor, as it should seem best to Him. And this took friction and anxiety out of his life in a very wonderful way."

CHAPTER SEVEN

THE CROSS AND PROPITIATION

The word *propitiation* comes from the root meaning mercy, or be merciful. The lid of the ark in the Holy of Holies in the tabernacle was the mercy seat, or propitiatory. The name *mercy seat* comes from the word for "atone," meaning to cover; and the mercy seat covered the ark, as well as the tables of the Law contained herein. The mercy seat was the place appointed by God for the meeting with Him in communion. In appointing, He said, "There I will meet with you, and I will speak with you from above the mercy seat" (Exodus 25:22).

The mercy seat was made of gold beaten out of the same piece as the cherubim, which represented the judgment of God, and these were placed at either end of the ark and looked down upon it. In the ark were placed the tables of the Law, and over it the cloud of glory rested. The cloud was the symbol of the presence of God, so that the ark was the throne of God in the midst of His people, for the tabernacle stood in the center of the camp of Israel.

It was on the mercy seat that the blood of the sin offering was sprinkled each year on the great Day of Atonement by the high priest. The blood spoke of a sacrifice having been made, on the ground of which God forgave the sins of His people. Being sprinkled before and on the mercy seat, it answered the claims of the Law within, which demanded death as the penalty for the breaking of the law.

By the blood, therefore, propitiation or satisfaction of the Law was effected, making it possible for God to bless the sinner in full accord with His righteousness. It had a twofold effect, procuring forgiveness of sins and giving access into the presence of God.

In Israel, the high priest alone had access into God's presence, and that only once a year on the Day of Atonement; and yet in entering into the Holy of Holies he acted as the representative of the people, so that all he did counted for them. The same ceremony had, however, to be repeated year by year, so that the offering up of the goat as a sacrifice, and the taking of its blood into the Holiest, showed that sin was not put away but remembered yearly. "For it is not possible that the blood of bulls and goats could take away sins"

(Hebrews 10:4); that could only be accomplished by the one great and perfect sacrifice offered once for all at Calvary. God, however, had in view that one sacrifice and so could forgive the sins of His people and give them a place before Him.

PROPITIATION DEFINED

Propitiation means to appease or satisfy wrath. God's righteous wrath against sin has been met and satisfied by the atoning work of Christ on the cross, for "He Himself is the propitiation for our sins, and not for ours only but also for the whole world" (1 John 2:2). God can never be indifferent to sin, nor can He pass over it lightly, for He is holy. Sin must be met and put away by death, if the blessing of God is to be received.

There are four references to the propitiation of Christ, and these are found in Romans, Hebrews, and 1 John. "Christ Jesus, whom God set forth as a propitiation by His blood, through faith, to demonstrate His righteousness, because in His forbearance God had passed over the sins that were previously committed" (Romans 3:24–25). This does not refer to the past sins of the believer but to the sins committed in Old Testament times, which were not put away but passed over by God through His forbearance in view of the propitiation to be made by Christ. The words "set forth" mean purposed, and remind us that the coming of Christ to suffer and die was God's purpose in a past eternity. The truth here presented is justification by faith.

Romans 1–3 show that all men are under sin and are guilty before God, deserving judgment; and that man therefore has no righteousness of his own. Then in verse 21 of chapter three the righteousness of God is proclaimed, which is a faith righteousness apart from works altogether, for it is a righteousness of God bestowed by Him on the believer. That righteousness can only be given after sin has been atoned for and put away; it is on the ground of the redemption in Christ.

THE EFFECT OF PROPITIATION

The work of Christ as a propitiation has so satisfied God's judgment upon sin that He cannot only forgive the sinner but can clear the most guilty and declare the believer righteous with the very righteousness of God. That is what *justified* means, and it is by faith and faith alone. By reason of that propitiation of Christ on the cross, God declares His righteousness in justifying the guilty one; for by it He dealt with sin, meeting it by death and enabling Him to act according to His own perfectly righteous character. It is that which makes the position of the believer so secure. No sin has been overlooked by God, but sin as guilt has been fully met, and every claim of God's holy law thereby answered. The work of Christ has perfectly satisfied God as regards sin, and He has borne witness thereto by raising Christ from the dead. That fact gives the believer true ground for peace with God (see Romans 5:1–2).

In the epistle to the Hebrews, the theme is the one perfect offering of Christ and His ministry as High Priest in the presence of God. In chapter one it is the glory of Christ as Son, by whom God has spoken. In chapter two it is Christ as man coming to give Himself an offering for sin and to stand before God on his behalf. Here is the second reference to the propitiation of Christ: He is a "merciful and faithful High Priest in things pertaining to God, to make propitiation for the sins of the people" (Hebrews 2:17). The incarnation of Christ was an absolute necessity if man's sin was to be met.

When God created man and woman, it was intended that they might walk in fellowship with God and be in such close touch with God that they should be able to govern the whole creation for God. But sin separated them from God and broke that happy fellowship. Sin must therefore be removed and mankind be brought back to God.

Hebrews shows how the one perfect sacrifice offered by Christ has put away sin and brought those who believe in Christ into the presence of God, and how they are kept there through the ministry of Christ as our High Priest. Particular emphasis is placed upon the blood of Christ, for it was by the blood that the high priest entered into the holiest. The veil that hung between the holy place and the Holy of Holies shut man out from the presence of God, and that veil was a type of Christ in the flesh. It was only when the veil was rent that free access to God was provided, and when Christ gave Himself on the cross and cried, "It is finished!" the veil was rent from top to bottom.

ACCESS TO GOD PROVIDED

The rending of the veil was the act of God by which He opened the way for any sinner to approach Him without fear, because of the blood of Christ. That was the new and living way made by God through the veil. Until the veil was rent, man was shut out from God's presence, and while Christ lived there was no access to God. However perfect Christ was as a man, and however perfect His teachings and His example, without the shedding of His blood there could be no access to God, nor communion with Him, for "without shedding of blood there is no remission" (Hebrews 9:22). But since His blood has been shed and the veil rent, none need stay out.

Christ is the propitiatory, or the Mercy Seat, where God meets everyone coming by faith in Christ. In entering into heaven itself to appear in the presence of God, Christ takes with Him all who become united to Him by faith. All who believe in Him are identified with Him. All He does is in a representative capacity on behalf of those who are His. Where He is, there are all who are His. "As He is, so are we in this world" (1 John 4:17).

FELLOWSHIP WITH GOD

The final references to the propitiation of Christ are in 1 John 2:2 and 4:10. Fellowship with God is the truth expounded in 1 John, for it concerns the believer as a child of God, and it is in the family relationship that fellowship is expressed. Fellowship is with God as light, as love, and as life. If fellowship is to be enjoyed, the believer must walk in the light, as God is in the light, because there is cleansing by the blood of Jesus (see 1 John 1:7).

Should sin be committed, fellowship is interrupted, but the advocacy of Christ avails. "And if anyone sins, we have an Advocate with the Father, Jesus Christ the righteous. And He Himself is the propitiation for our sins, and not for ours only but also for the whole world" (1 John 2:1–2). On account of His precious blood and His advocacy, there can be no condemnation for the believer who may sin.

Whenever a believer who has sinned confesses his sin, he is forgiven and cleansed. That means the restoration to communion with God as his Father. The propitiatory, or Mercy Seat was the place of communion or fellowship, and that is where all the children of God are brought by the blood of Jesus. Then by His advocacy as the High Priest in the presence of God, Christ maintains the believer in his relationship with the Father, and the one necessary condition in the life of the believer is the definite confession of his acts of sin. By naming the sin to God in a definite way, true confession is made.

GOD'S LOVING PROVISION

God demonstrated His love by sending Christ to be a propitiation for our sins, according to the apostle John. "In this is the love," John wrote, "that He loved us and sent His Son to be the propitiation for our sins" (1 John 4:10). In the previous verse, John told us that God's love was shown in His sending "His only begotten Son into the world, that we might live through Him." Christ's incarnation took place to meet each person's need under death and so bring life to each. But that could be accomplished only by sin's being propitiated, and so Jesus' death was required. The verses that follow refer to the believer's dwelling with God and His dwelling with us, and having His love perfected in us.

By the propitiation of Christ, we are brought to a better place than we could ever have enjoyed, even in innocence; for the work of Christ on the cross was not to restore men and women to Paradise as at the beginning. That place could be lost, and in fact was forfeited through sin; but believers in Christ are brought into oneness with God and to the very presence of God in the Holiest, a place which can never be lost. Our position there is determined by the work of Christ for Him at Calvary and by His high priestly ministry on our behalf. Our position before God is as perfect and eternal as the work and person of Christ can make His dwelling place in God Himself. (See, for instance, 1 John 4:16.)

An illustration of this truth is given in the case of the tax collector (Luke 18:13); for his prayer, "God be merciful to me a sinner," may well read, if translated literally, "God be propitious to me the sinner, on the ground of the shed blood"; that is the significance of the plea "be merciful." He came boldly to God, the Mercy Seat, and that with perfect honesty, acknowledging himself to be a sinner. His plea was the blood of Christ, one that God cannot refuse. It is His own provision, for access to His presence is available for the vilest and guiltiest. It is the will of God and His longing that all should come to Him and know the blessedness of living in holy and happy communion with Him.

The propitiation of Christ, therefore, has made it possible for every sinner to come to God and be at peace with Him. It has made the way of access into His presence open, so that He may be approached with boldness.

This should remove from the heart every doubt or fear, as well as every question regarding acceptance with God, and assure everyone coming in faith of the abiding favor and smile of God, continually and forever.

CHAPTER EIGHT

THE CROSS AND RECONCILIATION

ONE OF THE GREAT WORDS USED in connection with the work of the Cross of the Lord Jesus is *reconciliation*. The theme of Romans 5 is reconciliation, or a change effected by the Cross. Beyond Romans 5:10, the word *reconcile* in different forms is found in the following passages: Matthew 5:24; Acts 7:26; 2 Corinthians 5:18–20; Ephesians 2:16; and Colossians 1:20–21. From these Scriptures we get the unfolding of the truth.

The basis of the word is the Greek word *allatto* or *allasso*, meaning to change, found in other places with different prefixes. In Romans 1:25–26, it is "exchanged"; it is rendered "release" in Hebrews 2:15, "deliver" in Luke 12:58, and "went out" in Acts 19:12. The underlying thought in all of the words used is that of a change, for reconciliation means a change from a state of enmity, or estrangement, to one of peace and friendship. In 1 Corinthians 7:11, it is the coming together of husband and wife who have been separated; and in Romans 11:15, it is the change which was brought about in the world by the fall and casting away of Israel by God.

MEANING OF RECONCILIATION

Reconciliation then means a change from enmity to friendship, from estrangement and alienation to fellowship and nearness by the bringing about of a union. That is what is effected by the work of Christ.

Sin is enmity with God, and it estranges the sinner from God, and hinders any communion or friendship with Him. One of the characteristics of sin is hatred of God (see Romans 1:30), and sin is also hateful to God. Man naturally does not love God and trust Him with confidence, for that is the consequence of the Fall through sin. Even God's own people, the children of Israel, became estranged from God by breaking His law and by giving way to idolatry. They therefore incurred the wrath of God and were sold to other nations.

Throughout the Old Testament, when the wrath of God is referred to, it is almost in every instance directed against His own people or some servant of His, on account of disobedience to His Word, or refusal to conform to His will, and not at all against the heathen, or the nations who were ignorant to a large extent of His Word and His truth. The position of the heathen, or the nations, is described as being far off, aliens from the commonwealth of Israel, from the covenants of promise, without God and without any hope. But Israel as a nation was chosen as the channel of blessing and the custodian of the Word of God, which meant that all other peoples were dependent upon them for spiritual blessing and for the truth.

They had, however, so grievously departed from God that when the Lord Jesus came as their Messiah, they did not accept Him but rejected Him and called upon Pilate, the Roman governor, to crucify Him. By that act, therefore, they forfeited all claim to blessing for themselves and for any others through them. Not only so, but at the Cross the whole world took sides against God in rejecting His Son, so that all mankind, which was represented there, also forfeited any claim upon God, if there had been such.

But in giving Himself a willing offering and a sacrifice for sin, Christ met the wrath of God on account of sin, appeasing that wrath. Christ made it possible for God to meet man in grace and offer freely and abundantly every blessing that He has to bestow. By tearing the veil of the temple, He bore witness to this purpose, for that meant the opening up the way of access as it had never been done before.

The shedding of the blood of Christ opened the way into the presence of God for any and every sinner, however bad he might be. The Cross removed all that was between man and God, making it possible for man to come to God and become a friend. "God was in Christ reconciling the world to Himself, not imputing their trespasses to them" (2 Corinthians 5:19).

There—at the Cross—He put to the account of Christ the offenses against men and women as sinners, so that now He can reckon or impute to the guilty the righteousness of God. That is the truth of Romans 3 and 5, where guilty sinners are shown to be justified when they believe on Christ as Savior, and they are brought into a place where they can boast in God Himself through the Lord Jesus Christ.

PEACE WITH GOD ASSURED

The justified believer is brought into peace with God, or oneness with Him; he has access into the grace in which he stands; and he can boast of the hope of the glory of God, having received the reconciliation. God has become his closest friend, is entirely on his side, and will not hear any charge or accusation made against him—everything of that nature having been put to the account of Christ on the cross. From 2 Corinthians 5 we learn that the change is from a state of death to one of life and from the mere knowledge of Christ as a man to knowing Him as a risen and living Lord.

Because of this reconciliation, man becomes a new creature in Christ. The change is from his old position and old life into an entirely new place, everything having become new. The Cross has so changed the whole attitude of God, that man is urged to change his attitude from one of enmity to friendship. That is the appeal of the Gospel as proclaimed by those who are ambassadors for Christ. The enmity, even the law of commandments contained in ordinances, is abolished, according to Ephesians 2:15, and both Jew and Gentile are made one in Christ.

By the blood of Christ those who were far off and without God have been brought close to Him, for Christ is their peace, and in Him believers are made one with God. All estrangements and all differences between people are done away by the reconciling work of the Cross, for all who believe in Christ are made one new body. The position of all out of Christ is one of distance from God, but the Cross brings every believer near, giving access into His presence through the Spirit. In Colossians 1:20–21, the work of the Cross reconciles all those who were alienated and enemies by wicked works—who by their evil conduct showed their enmity. The reconciliation of Christ means that they will finally be presented to God holy, unblameable, and unreproveable. It means that wherever sin has made its power felt, there the work of the Cross reaches to remove its consequences and to bring peace and blessing.

It has been said that the Cross has made a platform on which God can offer freely to all people the fullest blessings, even to the vilest and guiltiest sinners. By the reconciling work of the Cross, God has shown Himself to be the friend of mankind, loving sinners and providing for them the fullest salvation and deliverance from sin and its power. Christ appeals to sinners to pull down the flag of opposition and enmity and come into that place of peace and friendship.

Peace means oneness, the removal of all conflict or strife, and the putting away of everything that could in any way separate or estrange one from another. In the peace offering described in Leviticus 3, the priest and the offerer, as well as God, received their portion on which all fed. This signified fellowship, for eating together is the symbol of fellowship throughout the Scriptures. It was offered as a thanksgiving to God also. Fellowship and thanksgiving are the outstanding ideas expressed by believers as they gather at the Lord's Table to break bread in remembrance of the Lord's death, looking forward to His coming again.

CHAPTER NINE

THE CROSS AND ATONEMENT

ATONEMENT IS AN OLD TESTAMENT word. The only place in the New Testament where it occurs in the King James Version is in Romans 5:11, and there it should be "reconciliation." The literal meaning of the word is covering and that is indicated by the first occurrence of the word in Genesis: "Cover it inside and outside with pitch" (6:14). The covering of the ark with pitch was for the sake of safety. However perfectly it was built in obedience to the instructions given by God, the ark would not have been safe unless it had that covering. The pitch made it safe as a refuge from the waters of the flood. As the pitch made the ark a safe refuge from judgment by the flood, even so atonement means safety from judgment. By atonement the believer is made safe from the judgement of God on account of sin, and that atonement is blood (Leviticus 17:11).

Other words that are translations of the Hebrew word for "atonement" include *reconcile, purge, ransom, forgive, satisfaction, be merciful, appease,* and *put away.* The phrase "mercy seat" comes from the word *atone,* for it was the covering over the ark in the Holy of Holies. It was the lid of the ark, covering the tables of the Law, which were placed in the ark. The cherubim, placed at either end of the ark, were beaten out of the same piece of gold as the lid and represented the judgment of God against sin. Looking down on the ark and into it, they could see the Law there, but the sprinkled blood on the mercy seat spoke to them of judgment fulfilled by the sacrifice.

On the great Day of Atonement, which came round yearly, the high priest took the blood of the sin offering into the Holiest and sprinkled it before and on the mercy seat. It was over the mercy seat that the Shechinah cloud rested, making it the throne of God in the midst of His people. The blood sprinkled there witnessed to the sacrifice for sin which had been offered and an atonement made for the sins of the people so that God could dwell among them.

On the tenth day of the seventh month of each year, the high priest took two goats and standing before the tabernacle cast lots for them. The one on which the lot for Jehovah fell was offered in sacrifice, and the other was a scapegoat. The goat for Jehovah was sacrificed at the brazen altar and its blood taken into the holiest place and sprinkled as mentioned; then the high priest went to the door of the tabernacle and, laying both of his hands on the head of the live goat, confessed over it all the sin, iniquities, and transgressions of the people and sent it away into the wilderness by a suitable person.

THE SCAPEGOAT: A TYPE OF CHRIST

The scapegoat was the goat of departure, for that is evidently the meaning of the word *scape*. The goat sacrificed speaks of expiation for sin; and the goat sent away of conciliation, signifying the removal of sins from the people. The sole ground of forgiveness was atonement made by sacrifice, which was to satisfy the claims of God's holy law. That having been done, the sins of the people were removed by being confessed over the live goat.

That type will find its fulfillment when the Lord Jesus comes forth from the presence of God and when Israel as a nation turns to Him in confession and their sins are taken away entirely. That is what is described in Zechariah 12:10–14 and is the explanation of Romans 11:26–27. The meaning of the type is given in Hebrews 9:24–28, describing the three appearings of Christ. He appeared at the altar and offered Himself a sacrifice (v. 26); then He went into the presence of God and now appears there for us (v. 24); and the day is coming when He will appear without sin unto salvation (v. 28).

The appearance of Christ mentioned in Hebrews 9:28 is that coming to the earth when He will manifest Himself to Israel, and not His coming into the air as described in 1 Thessalonians 4:13–18. It is the only time that the word "second" is used in connection with His advent. According to the typical teaching in Leviticus 16, it is for Israel. In that chapter, Aaron is said to offer a bull "for himself and for his house" (vv. 6 and 11); the blood of that bull was carried by him into the Holiest, and so atonement was made. There was no scape-bull as in the case of the scapegoat offered later.

The expression "for his house" is peculiar to this passage, being found nowhere else, and it points to atonement made for believers who belong to the church, as distinguished from Israel for whom the goat was offered, for Aaron's sons typify believers as a priesthood. The coming out of the priest was the witness to the children of Israel that their sins had been atoned for; and then by the action of the priest with the scapegoat, they were put away from them. In contrast with that, we who believe have the witness of the Holy Spirit (Hebrew 10:15). The presence of the Holy Spirit in every believer is the witness to him that Christ arose and ascended to the right hand of God, that his sins are put away entirely, and that God has accepted Christ fully on his behalf.

Just as the people of Israel waited at the tabernacle door for the priest to appear and then confess their sins over the live goat, so that nation now awaits the coming of Christ as its Messiah. When He appears, according Zechariah 12:10 and 14:4; and Revelation 1:7, that nation will turn to Him; "so all Israel will be saved" (Romans 11:26).

By His death on the cross and the shedding of His blood, Christ made full atonement for sin. Even though the word *atonement* is not used in the New Testament in connection with the work of the Cross, the truth is unfolded in the epistle to the Hebrews in connection with His one perfect sacrifice, followed by His high priestly work in the presence of God. As has been mentioned, the work of the high priest on the Day of Atonement is the type referred to in Hebrews 9. The one perfect sacrifice of Christ offered once for all is contrasted with the many sacrifices under the law, which were continually repeated, showing that sin was not put away, whereas Christ put away sin by the sacrifice of Himself.

SIN PUT AWAY BY ONE SACRIFICE

The Old Testament sacrifices did not abolish sin; they could not take away sins entirely (Hebrews 10:4, 11). But what they failed to do has been done completely by the one sacrifice of Christ. The old sacrifices were for the purifying of the flesh, whereas the one perfect sacrifice of Christ purges the conscience, so that the believer has "no more conscience of sins."

The blood of the sin offering on the Day of Atonement made it possible for the high priest to enter the Holy of Holies through the veil, but that was only once a year. When Christ shed His blood at the cross, the veil was rent and the way opened for every believer to enter the Holiest at all times without fear or doubt, but with all boldness. Access the presence of God through the rent veil was something that no Israelite ever knew or could possibly know.

God's decree was "It is the blood that makes atonement for the soul" (Leviticus 17:11), and that must be the blood of a sinless victim. When the blood is in view as an atonement, it means blood shed, or poured out. The expression "for the blood is the life" (Deuteronomy 12:23) does not mean the blood coursing through the veins of a living being, but the blood by death. Death is the penalty for sin, and no sin can be put away except by death. As long as the veil hung in the tabernacle or in the temple, it shut man out from the presence of God, and only after the veil was rent could there be unhindered access to Him.

The word *veil* means to divide or rend, and its name had the significance of rending. The veil spoke wonderfully of the flesh of Christ, pointing to Him as a man, God incarnate. However great and beautiful He was as a man, however wonderful as a teacher and leader, and however blessed as an example, apart from the shedding of His blood, He could not bring one person to God. His blood had to be shed if He were to open the way into the presence of God.

The more perfect and wonderful He is represented by teachers and others, the more does He shut men out of God's presence, unless His atoning blood is accepted and relied upon for salvation. "Without shedding of blood there is no remission"; none whatever! But because of the shedding of that precious blood of Christ, there is full and absolute forgiveness of all sins, and that forever. When sins have been put away by the sacrifice of Christ, they are blotted out and forgotten forever.

ONE PERFECT COVERING FOR SIN

God's covering for sin is perfect. From the beginning, people have tried to cover up their sins without any success. Adam and Eve tried to cover up theirs. Joseph's brothers thought that their crime would be forgotten, but after twenty years it came up again and convicted them. By hiding the wedge of gold and the Babylonian garment in his tent, Achan thought to cover up his sin, but it was found out. God's Word to the two and a half tribes, "Be sure your sin will find you out" (Numbers 32:23), ever comes true for every individual.

God is the only one who can cover up sin, and His covering is the only one that will avail if we are to stand before Him accepted and forgiven. It is the blood of Jesus and that alone that can cleanse the sinner from a single sin and make it possible for him to come to God and find acceptance. "The blood of Jesus Christ His Son cleanses us from *all sin*" (1 John 1:7, italics added).

Not only was the sacrifice made once for all, providing atonement for sin, but it is continually effective. Atonement by the blood of Christ has made atonement for all sin—past, present, and future. It puts the believer in a place of continual acceptance or continuous blessing. The word "continually" in Hebrews 7:3 and 10:1 is rendered "forever" in Hebrew 10:12, 14 and means uninterrupted continuance.

There were constant changes in the high priests in Old Testament times on account of death, but the priesthood of Christ is unchangeable. There can be no break in His priestly work, even for a moment. And the same continuance is connected with His sacrifice. The Old Testament sacrifices were offered "continually year by year," showing their imperfection; "but this Man after He had offered one sacrifice for sins forever, sat down" (Hebrews 10:12). His sacrifice was forever, and so there is no break in its efficacy. From the moment that a believer accepts it for his sins, continually he is safe. Its efficacy is continuous, so that a person has ever a place in the sight of God and access into His presence. Moreover, the believer is "perfected forever," or continuously. His standing before God is perfect and that forever. Nothing that he may ever do can disturb his standing before God a moment, for it is determined by that one perfect offering given forever.

The believer's salvation, his acceptance by God, and his presence before God in the Holiest, are secured by that one perfect sacrifice of the Lord Jesus at Calvary when He shed His precious blood for sinners. That is the full significance of atonement by the blood of Christ. For all eternity it will be through the efficacy of the blood of Christ that every believer will have a place in the holy presence of God the Father and of Christ. The word atonement is sometimes spelled "At-one-ment," as if that is what the word signifies; but that is a mistake, as will readily be seen from what has been said as to its true meaning—a covering. Peace means oneness, which comes only as the result of the atonement made by the blood.

CHAPTER TEN

THE CROSS AND
SUBSTITUTION

IN OBEDIENCE TO THE CALL of God, Abraham offered to sacrifice his only son. God responded to Abraham's faith by providing a ram in place of Isaac as an offering. The concept of substitution is wonderfully illustrated in this encounter in Genesis 22. This event typified Christ's substitutionary work to come.

Although *substitution* is not a biblical term, its truth is prominent in the Scriptures of both Old and New Testaments.

In Isaiah 53, a chapter which occupies a remarkable place in that book, *substitution* finds expression fourteen times. Toward the beginning of the chapter there a seven statements, and toward the end of the chapter another seven, all bringing out the truth of substitution. "Surely He has borne our griefs and carried our sorrows . . . He was wounded for our transgressions, He was bruised for our iniquities; the chastisement for our peace was upon Him, and by His stripes we are healed. . . . And the Lord has laid on Him the iniquity of us all" (vv. 4–6).

From verse 8 to the end of that chapter there are several other statements, as follows: "For the transgressions of My people He was stricken. . . . You [will] make His soul an offering for sin. . . . . By His knowledge My righteous Servant shall justify many, for He shall bear their iniquities. . . . He was numbered with the transgressors, and He bore the sin of many, and made intercession for the transgressors" (vv. 8, 10–12).

Isaiah 53 is the middle chapter of the last section of the book, containing chapters 40–66. These twenty-seven chapters of Isaiah divide into three sections, having chapters 49–57 as the central part with chapter 53 as the middle one of that central section. Right in the center of the chapter (v. 7) are the words "He was led as a lamb to the slaughter." All of these predictions were wonderfully fulfilled at the cross of Christ, when the Messiah offered Himself on behalf of sinners and gave Himself a ransom for many.

Notice has been taken of the different passages where Christ is said to have died for others, and it has been shown the word *for* typically signifies "on behalf of." However, in Matthew 20:28 and Mark 10:45, where His coming "to give His life a ransom *for many*" are the words used, the word "for" means instead of, for it is the Greek word *anti*. In 1 Timothy 2:6 there is almost the very same expression, only instead of the word "many" it is "all", and the word "for" is not *anti* but *uper*—"on behalf of"; so the perfect accuracy of the Scriptures is evident. He gave Himself to provide a ransom "on behalf of all," but it was "instead of" the many, not of all, for all do not accept the sacrifice.

CHRIST, THE SINNER'S SUBSTITUTE

Christ, therefore, was a substitute for all who believe in Him as their Savior. It was when He hung on the cross that He became the substitute and not during His life. "The Lord has laid on Him the iniquity of us all" (Isaiah 53:6). He suffered, "the just for the unjust." He willingly took the place of the guilty sinner and bore the judgment of sin, that the sinner who believes on Him might not only be pardoned and cleared of his guilt and its judgment but become the righteousness of God in Him.

When Abraham offered the ram on the altar, Isaac was unbound and set free; and he owed his life to the substitution of the ram and its sacrifice. One of the strongest statements showing what the Cross meant to Christ is in 2 Corinthians 5:21: "He made Him . . . sin for us." Then Paul stated in Galatians 3:13 that Christ was made a curse for us. While these passages and other similar ones mean that it was on behalf of others that

He died on the cross and gave His life, still the context shows that the truth of substitution is contained in most of them.

"He died for all, that those who live should no longer live for themselves, but for Him who died for them and rose again" (2 Corinthians 5:15).

"Who gave Himself for us, that He might redeem us from every lawless deed" (Titus 2:14).

"Who Himself bore our sins in His own body on the tree, that we, having died to sins, might live for righteousness" (1 Peter 2:24).

"Christ also suffered once for sins, the just for the unjust, that He might bring us to God" (1 Peter 3:18).

All of these passages clearly indicate the two sides of substitution: Christ is put in the place of the sinner, bearing his guilt and judgment, and the believer in consequence is blessed, as indicated by the word "that."

All that sin meant to the sinner as guilt, condemnation, judgment, and punishment was borne by Christ. He took the place of the sinner and bore all that was against each sinner to the full. Thus anyone believing on Him is fully absolved from his or her sin and guilt and becomes the righteousness of God in Christ. Whether sin be represented as guilt, or a debt, or a burden, or condemnation, all were put to Christ, and His death on the cross met all that was demanded by God on account of sin.

RECEIVING HIS RIGHTEOUSNESS

And then there is the other side, which is apt to be overlooked in the joy that comes from seeing one's sin put away. It is the place that the believer is put in when Christ is accepted as Savior. Instead of his sin being put upon him, he is clothed with the righteousness of God in Christ and he becomes the righteousness of God in Christ. This is indicated by the word "that." Christ died and the believer lives, having eternal life, "*that* we, having died to sins, might live for righteousness" (1 Peter 2:24). He was condemned as guilty *that* we might be accepted as righteous. He took our place *that* we might be put in His. He bore the curse *that* the blessing of God might be ours. He cried, "My God, My God, why have You forsaken Me," that we should never be forsaken by God, even for a moment, for His word to the believer is "I will never leave you nor forsake you."

The believer in Christ becomes in the sight of God all that Christ was and is. Christ Himself is our righteousness, our sanctification, and our redemption. The substitution of Christ for us is wonderful—being all of grace; yet many are slow to understand it or realize its fullness. The more the believer recognizes the awful depths to which Christ went when He suffered for him, and what His going to the cross cost Him, the more that believer will enter into the meaning of Jesus' death and find that it takes him to the other extreme. Jesus went down to the very lowest place that He might lift us into the very highest place it is possible for God to give any being. From the throne in heaven He stooped to the humiliating death of a malefactor at Golgotha that every believer might be exalted to His throne of glory.

A SUBSTITUTE FOR BARABBAS

At the very time that Christ was suffering on the cross, a guilty sinner was taken out of his place of condemnation, pardoned, and given his freedom. That man was Barabbas, the guilty robber and murderer. He was awaiting death as the penalty of his crime, knowing that it was just judgment for what he had done. But he was released by the Roman governor and set free from his punishment because Christ took his place. He knew he was guilty and deserved death as his punishment. Doubtless, he knew that Jesus was innocent and did not merit death. It was evidently the very cross prepared for Barabbas on which the Lord Jesus suffered.

Of all the people in Jerusalem that day when Jesus was crucified, Barabbas could have truthfully said, "That man is in my place; He is dying in my stead." And the law could never afterwards lay its hand on Barabbas and arrest him for his crime, for by the cross of Christ, it was settled forever. This was all of grace, for Barabbas knew only too well that he had done absolutely nothing to merit such a pardon and freedom, but rather that according to the law it should have been the very opposite.

The place that Barabbas occupied is the very place that God would have every sinner take, and in simple faith look at the cross and say from the very depths of his heart, "That Man is in my place." We can imagine Barabbas going home to his friends and their amazement when they saw that he was free. All he could say by way of explanation was one word, "*Jesus*—Jesus took my place, and I am free."

In writing to Philemon, the apostle Paul gives an illustration of this truth by saying that he would have retained Onesimus to minister to him instead of Philemon. Later on in his letter, he requests Philemon to put to his account any wrong done by Onesimus, and he would repay it.

"HE DIED FOR ME"

The truth of substitution is illustrated in history by the conscript's substitute. On one occasion when a man with a family was conscripted for the army, a lad came forward and offered to go in his stead. His offer was accepted, and he went as a substitute. He was killed in action, so that man in whose stead he went could say, "He died for me." Other instances of a similar nature have been given, and while they illustrate one side of substitution, they fail the other; for the one taking the penalty cannot put the other fully in the place of righteousness. "He made Him who knew no sin to be sin for us, that we might become the righteousness of God in Him" (2 Corinthians 5:21).

A. T. Pierson, in his book *God's Living Oracles*, showed that the principle of substitution is not absolutely new. He wrote,

> In human society [substitution] has always been an admitted principle; as, for instance, in war. The story of the Napoleonic campaigns is familiar to all, how in early wars a man was drafted, in France, and, being unable to go to the field himself, hired a substitute and paid a good price for him, who went to the war, and fell on one of the battlefields. In a subsequent draft, the same man was drafted again. He went to the recruiting office and produced his papers, proving that he had hired and paid for a substitute, who had died on the battlefield; and the entry was accordingly made against his name: "Died in the person of his substitute on the battlefield of Rivoli." The believer, standing before a violated law, as one who has found in Jesus Christ his substitute, may claim immunity from the desert of his sin; he may boldly affirm, "I died in the person of the Lord Jesus Christ, on the battlefield of Calvary over nineteen hundred years ago" (See 2 Corinthians 5:15; Romans 6:1-8). That is salvation. That is redemption.

Pierson then told a second true story, this one set in an American school for boys. A well-known teacher there let the students make the rules for their own government and determined the various penalties for violating the rules.

> One little fellow, however, more than once violated the law, and became liable to a flogging. He was called up, according to the rules of the boys themselves, to have the rod laid on his back. Just then the door of the school opened, and in came his elder brother, who, taking in the whole situation at a glance, said to the master: "Would you have any objection to my taking the whipping for my brother?"
>
> "Do you think, boys, the honor of the school and its laws would be sufficiently upheld?" was the teacher's appeal.
>
> They held up their hands, whereupon the brother bared his back and took the whipping instead of the offender. The principle of substitution was again illustrated.

Pierson related another touching story he heard and its application to the principle of substitution:

> [During] the war between Russia and Circassia in the middle of the [nineteenth] century, the prophet chief Schamyl, almost adored by his followers, found that someone was exposing to the enemy his designs

and plans; and so he made a decree, which he promulgated to his followers, that if the traitor were found out, one hundred lashes on the bare back should be administered for the offense.

A few days later, it was discovered to his astonishment, that the guilty party was his own mother. He went into fasting and retirement for two days, and coming out pallid and ghastly, ordered his mother to be brought from the tent and her back bared for the scourge. He stood by while one, two, three, four, five of those fearful lashes gashed her flesh; then he bade the executioner arrest his blows, bared his own back, and took the other ninety-five lashes on his own person until the flesh hung in shreds.

The effect, it is said, was electric—his followers were melted, and even his mother was utterly subdued, as she never would have been by mere force. The exhibition of vicarious love, and of the principle of substitution and satisfaction, accomplished all desirable ends more effectively than the full penalty executed on the offender.

Thus the principle of substitution is not entirely foreign to humanity, and the beauty and power of it have many a time been acknowledged, even in the circles of society.

Alas! and did my Saviour bleed,
And did my Sovereign die?
Would He devote that sacred head
For such a worm as I?

Was it for crimes that I have done,
He groaned upon the tree?
Amazing pity! Grace unknown!
And love beyond degree!

—Isaac Watts

CHAPTER ELEVEN

THE CROSS AND IDENTIFICATION

THE CROSS, AS IT APPLIES TO the Christian in his or her life, has received notice in previous chapters, but the truth of the identification of the believer with Christ in His death and resurrection is of such importance as to deserve a fuller unfolding.

In His incarnation, the Lord Jesus identified Himself with people. He did so that He might stand for them and meet their needs under sin and death. In permitting John the Baptist to baptize Him, and thus putting Himself in the place of death and burial—for that is what baptism means—He had in view His death for sinners, placing Himself under the judgment of God due to sin. In the same way, the believer in his baptism identifies himself with Christ in death, burial, and resurrection. This truth is brought out in Romans 6, where sin is recognized as a master or tyrant, even over believers; but that rule or dominion is nullified by the constant reckoning of oneself dead unto sin and alive unto God.

The words of Colossians 2:10–12 bring out the same truth, where the completeness of the position of the believer is opened up. There it is revealed that the body of the sins of flesh has been cut off—the believer having been buried with Him in baptism. Christ not only died for our sins but He died to sin, and by His resurrection He was delivered from sin entirely and forever, and can never again by any possibility come under sin or its judgment. By His death and resurrection sin's power was broken, and now all that Christ accomplished on the cross is imputed to the believer, who is looked upon as one with Christ in His finished work.

Christ acted in a representative way in His work, so that He did and does count for those who are His. The application of this truth is by faith alone; or, as it is put in Romans 6:11, "Reckon yourselves to be dead indeed to sin, but alive to God in Christ Jesus our Lord." The reckoning is on the ground of the position of the believer made possible by the work of Christ, and baptism is evidence of its being known (v. 3). The reckoning is followed by yielding the members of the body to God (v. 13), and then by obedience (v. 16), for these are the conditions which make the experience of the believer accord with his position. The results are freedom from sin's mastery, holiness in life, and fruitfulness in service.

DEAD TO THE LAW

The same argument is applied in Romans 7 to the relation of the believer to the Mosaic Law. At the cross Christ satisfied all claims that the Law had against the sinner because of its having been broken; and there He blotted out the bond that was against him, written in ordinances; He nailed the bond to the cross (see Colossians 2:14). Believers are therefore become dead to the law by the body of Christ, that they should be married to another, that is, be subject to Him who is raised from the dead and be under His control and rule. That is the secret of deliverance from all legality and from the power of the flesh itself. By identification with Christ in death and resurrection, the believer rises to newness of life, to walk in newness of spirit (Romans 6:4; 7:6; Galatians 5:16, 25).

"Crucified with Christ" is another expression, prominent in Galatians, where freedom from all legality—and all rites and rules of an outward nature in which the flesh would find something to glory—is emphasized. That epistle teaches that God will not accept any personal effort at all for either our justification or sanctification, for every blessing is granted freely to faith by grace. Those who are Christ's have been crucified to the world and the world to them; and they are thus separated from the old life in the flesh and committed to a new life in Christ by faith (Galatians 2:20).

Israel's separation from their old life in Egypt, when brought out and taken through the Red Sea, typifies the position of the believer—the Red Sea representing the Cross of Christ. Worldliness, therefore, in a believer's life means the denial of the Cross and his oneness with Christ, as one redeemed by His death. "Those who are Christ's have crucified the flesh with its passions and desires" (Galatians 5:24).

RESURRECTION LIFE

The resurrection of Christ is always connected with His death, for apart from the resurrection of His body His death would be valueless; and that includes the ascension of His body to the right hand of God. The body of Christ was raised from the dead by the Holy Spirit, and the believer is quickened together with Him by the sovereign grace of God (Ephesians 2:5; Colossians 2:13). The quickening was the raising up of the body into resurrection life, for it is resurrection life that is imparted when the sinner believes on Christ, accepting Him as Savior and Lord. That is what the new birth means (John 1:12).

Resurrection is an act of God, and it is through faith in the operation of God that believers are raised, so that their position is oneness with Christ in His finished work (Colossians 2:12–13). The blessedness of that position will be realized by those who have their affections set on things above and not on things on the earth, recognizing that they are dead and that their life is hidden with Christ in God, and that Christ Himself is their very life (Colossians 3:1–4).

All believers are raised together and are seated together in heavenly places in Christ Jesus (Ephesians 2:6); and so the full value of the work of Christ in His death, resurrection, and ascension is reckoned to the believer. These great acts are counted as having been performed in the very lives of those who are joined to Christ by faith. God in His sovereign grace has not only made these blessings free, but also full and abundant.

IDENTIFICATION WITH CHRIST

There are other expressions where this truth of identification with Christ is brought out, which present other aspects of Christian life and experience. Children of God are made heirs of an inheritance and are joint heirs with Christ (Romans 8:17). This is connected with their joint suffering with Him in this present life. The sufferings are in view of the coming glory, for we shall also be glorified with Him, sharing the very glory given Him by His Father. That will be when the manifestation of believers as children of God takes place at the coming of Christ and the redemption procured by His blood is realized. It will be then that all believers will receive their redeemed bodies, which will never be subject to pain or sickness or any failure or sin. That is what the children of God hope for with joyful faith, "waiting for the adoption" (Romans 8:23). And finally, there will be the reigning with Him as the reward of enduring in this present time (2 Timothy 2:12). *Endurance* means bearing up under burdens, trials and afflictions, and hence has the idea of suffering, but the word means more than suffering, for enduring implies victory.

The position of each believer in his identification with Christ is presented by the words "dead with," "buried with," "crucified with"; then "made alive together with Him," "raised up with Him," and "made to sit with Him in the heavenlies"—all pointing to what is accomplished and perfect, the work of God in Christ. At present, Christians are granted the privilege of suffering with Him, as is realized by those who identify themselves with Him as a rejected Savior and Lord (Acts 5:41; Philippians 1:29). In the future, all such are to live with Him (Romans 6:8; 2 Timothy 2:11; 1 Peter 4:13) and also to reign with Him in His coming glorious kingdom.

THE RED HEIFER TYPE

One Old Testament type in particular presents this truth of identification with Christ, its teaching being connected with the position of the believer in the world. It is the offering of the red heifer in Numbers

19. That sacrifice was appointed by God as the provision for the cleansing of anyone in Israel who might become defiled by coming in touch with a dead body while traveling through the wilderness. The ordinance appointed that a red heifer should be taken—without spot or blemish, one that had never been under the yoke—and then slain outside the camp. Its blood was to be sprinkled before the tabernacle seven times and the whole animal burnt, together with cedar wood, scarlet, and hyssop. The ashes were to be kept in a clean place, to be used for a water of separation. When anyone became defiled, those ashes were to be taken and put with running water, and then on the third and seventh days sprinkled with hyssop on the person defiled and on whatever object had become unclean. After that, when the person had washed his clothes and bathed himself, he was clean.

That was the only occasion on which a red heifer was offered. In other passages where a heifer is mentioned as a sacrifice, the word is different, sometimes being rendered "calf." The word *red* is the same as *adam* in the Hebrew, and so points to that which is human. It typified Christ in His incarnation. The heifer had to be without spot, or perfect—with no blemish whatever. It was faultless. It also had to have never been under the yoke and so free from all subjection or discipline. There was no need for any yoke in the case of Christ; but all others, free from such restraint, act in self-will, which is sin.

When a female was allowed for an offering, it was for the people; but a priest, or ruler, or the whole congregation had to bring a male bull. The root of the word for heifer, being "fruitfulness" or "increase," implying life, is significant. The sacrifice presents Christ as identified with man in order to provide the one perfect and complete offering. The burning of the cedar wood, hyssop, and scarlet, along with the whole animal, shows the identification of the believer with Christ in His sacrifice under the judgment of God.

Solomon "spoke of the trees, from the cedar tree of Lebanon even to the hyssop that springs out of the wall" (1 Kings 4:33). These are the greatest and the least of the plant world, and so stand for men of all ranks of life. Scarlet clothing, or that which was double dyed, meant luxury and comfort, and so pointed to the glory of man; for man at his very best must come to the place of sacrifice, which speaks of death and of judgment, if he is to have any dealings with God or any standing before Him. The only other place where cedar wood and scarlet and hyssop were connected with an offering was the case of the cleansing of the leper (Leviticus 14) and his restoration to the camp when clean.

ASHES AND RESURRECTION

Ashes speak of resurrection, and they were kept as a memorial of the one offering made once for all and were to be used for a water of separation for purification from sin. The word "separation" is used in Leviticus 12 and 15 (KJV), and in Numbers 19 (KJV) in connection with uncleanness in the flesh; and the word "purification" occurs in other passages as sin and the sin offering. Throughout the Scriptures water is a type of the Word, and running or living water refers to the Holy Spirit. These two ever work in unison and never apart.

THE SPRINKLED BLOOD

When the children of Israel sprinkled the blood on the doorposts at the time of the Passover, they used a bunch of hyssop, a common weed growing round about their houses and so within the reach of everyone. The sprinkling of the blood always means the appropriation of the sacrifice by faith. As has been noticed, the believer in his identification with Christ enters into all that His sacrifice on the cross meant, and so is fully and forever absolved from the guilt of sin and its judgment. But through defilement he loses communion with God, and that robs his service and testimony of power and effect.

In this type, the provision is seen for the cleansing of the believer and his restoration to fellowship and blessing. The washing of the disciples' feet on the night of the Passover by the Lord Jesus (John 13) teaches and illustrates this truth, and it shows how necessary it is for one to be clean, if he is to have any part with Him.

When the Word of God and the Spirit of God are given their rightful place in the life of the believer, sin will be readily detected, and then these will point him to the provision made for cleansing and forgiveness. "If we confess our sins, He is faithful and just to forgive us our sins and to cleanse us from all unrighteousness" (1 John 1:9). These are procured by the advocacy of Christ and realized in experience when there is confession. Confession of sin is not asking to be forgiven but is acknowledging the act of commission or of omission as sin, and that in a definite way. Christians will find that the very naming of a sin or a shortcoming as sin is a deterrent in the future.

CHAPTER TWELVE

THE CROSS A TEST

*T*HERE IS A DAY OF JUDGMENT coming when every saint must stand before God for approval or disapproval. While the believer in Christ will not come into judgment for sin as guilt, he will have to answer for his conduct and for all service rendered or not rendered as a Christian; it will not be so much a time of trial or testing but the passing of God's sentence of approval or disapproval. The present life is the time of trial when people are being proved, and it is declared that those who do not believe on the Lord Jesus Christ are condemned already (John 3:18), for they refuse the light and turn from it in unbelief. The judgment seat of Christ will be a time of approval or of disapproval, bringing reward or loss to those who are saved. At present, believers as well as unbelievers are being tested or tried, and their manner of conduct and service will determine the sentence passed upon them.

No sooner had humans been created and placed in the very best of surroundings, with everything to minister to their enjoyment and comfort as well as to help them to fulfill all responsibilities from God, than they were tempted by the devil; and the whole race has since learned the awful consequences of the Fall that then took place. All the ruin and misery that have been realized by mankind have been the result of yielding to the temptation in the Garden of Eden by doubting the word of God. And yet that temptation which God permitted was most wise and good. There cannot be a truly strong and useful life apart from testing.

Testings are allowed so that all that is strong and good may be approved and found to be reliable and trustworthy. Temptation is not permitted for the purpose of causing an individual to fall but in order that he may be strengthened and so approve himself. God's dealings with men and women are in view of eternity and not for time. The present life, therefore, is a time of testing, when those at school are being prepared for the eternal state. That is essentially true of believers, for the Gospel, which brings salvation to believers, points to the future and gives a blessed and living hope.

THE WORLD TESTED

The one great test is the Cross of Christ. There the world was tested and sadly failed. At the cross the world took sides against God, and by rejecting the Son of God and putting Him to a shameful death manifested its guilt and deserved judgment of God. "Now is the judgment of this world; now the ruler of this world will be cast out" (John 12:31), are the words which came from the lips of the Lord Jesus, when announcing His death. The Cross was the culmination of all tests under which man was placed, and his absolute failure there showed that the very best of mankind have no standing before God. Among those who united in the crucifixion of Christ, all classes of people were represented, from the highest to the lowest. The representatives of the government, the religious leaders, and the common people all combined to reject and crucify the Son of God. If anyone had any claim upon God, it was rejected there; and in consequence, everyone is shut up to the grace of God for blessing, which means that only through the merits of Christ can there be any acceptance by God.

The Cross tests people in regard to life, doctrine, and service. As the first need of man is light, doctrine should doubtless be put first. For all life and service are dependent upon truth and teaching. "In Him was life, and the life was the light of men" (John 1:4). In the Christian's experience, light comes through life, or living out what is learned. Eternal life is received as a gift by faith, and faith rests upon the Word of God being heard in the Gospel and its teaching.

DOCTRINES FOUNDED UPON THE CROSS

All doctrine is founded upon the Cross, and all the great truths that appeal to faith find expression there. It is there that we learn about God and see His character manifested in all its fullness. There His holiness, His wisdom, His love, and His power are shown forth; and only as we come to the Cross in faith can we really know the truth that "God is love" (1 John 4:8). "By this we know love, because He laid down His life for us" (1 John 3:16). "In this is love, not that we loved God, but that He loved us and sent His Son to be the propitiation for our sins" (1 John 4:10). His holiness and righteousness were manifested there in His hatred of sin, and in His judgment of it in giving His Son as a sacrifice for it. "He . . . did not spare His own Son, but delivered Him up for us all" (Romans 8:32). In meeting all the forces of evil there, destroying the devil, and abolishing death, He showed forth His omnipotence as well as His wisdom and grace.

The whole truth regarding Christ as the Son of God is borne witness to at the Cross. The fact that He died is evidence of His humanity; and therefore that He went there on behalf of mankind. The cries that went up from the Lord Jesus, and the wonderful events which took place as He yielded up His spirit, convinced some who stood round the cross that He was indeed the Son of God. It established the great truth that He was God incarnate—God manifest in the flesh. Prophecies uttered hundreds of years before were so literally fulfilled in the death of Christ that it demonstrated the truth of the Word of God, attested those prophecies as divinely given, and proved that the very words of the prophets were inspired by the Spirit of God.

The experiences given with such detail in Psalms 22 and 69 and the truths enunciated in Isaiah 53 cannot be truly understood except as they are read and interpreted in the light of the Cross. All the great doctrines relating to salvation and the Christian life are based upon the finished work of Christ in His sacrificial and atoning death. And when one looks forward to the future and the coming judgment, whether a believer or an unbeliever, it is the Cross of Christ that settles the question as to one's acceptance or his awful condemnation. If there is no such thing as eternal punishment as the judgment of God upon the impenitent sinner, why did Christ suffer such awful agony as He did on the cross?

But the Cross witnesses to the heinousness of sin, to its vileness and damnableness, showing that no punishment can be too terrible for such dastardly actions and such inexcusable malice and madness. The utter depravity of man, his awful hatred of God, and therefore of that which is good, as well as his helplessness to do good, are clearly exhibited in the crucifixion of the Son of God. The attitude of everyone to the Cross shows their position in regard to truth and to the doctrines of the Word of God.

Only as we test our beliefs by the Cross of Christ can we be sure of our standing before God and know what our destiny will be. In these days of apostasy and awful departure from the Word of God, and the consequent rejection of truth, there is greater need than ever to test all teaching that comes to us by the standard given by God in the Cross of Christ.

MAN'S GREAT NEED—LIFE

Apart from Christ there is no true life, for all men naturally are dead in sin. It is in Him that we have eternal life, for "he who has the Son has life; he who does not have the Son of God does not have not life" (1 John 5:12). He came to give life to the world, for He said, "I have come that they may have life, and that they may have it more abundantly" (John 10:10). "In Him was life, and the life was the light of men" (John 1:4). These passages plainly show that it is in Christ alone that life is to be found, and *that* life is an abundant one.

One of the great key words of the gospel of John is "life", for he states at the close of his gospel that it was written to prove that Jesus was the Christ, the Son of God, so that all who believe on Him might have life in His name. Eternal life is the free gift of God through Jesus Christ our Lord. It is by receiving Christ that life is received, and those who believe on Christ become children of God (John 1:12–13). That means coming to the Cross and recognizing His death as the answer to our sin and its only remedy, and receiving Him as Lord.

There can be no union with Christ save through death, which is the one and only answer to sin. When one comes to the Cross, he comes to the end of the old life and receives the new life in Christ. "I have been crucified with Christ . . . and the life which I now live in the flesh I live by faith in the Son of God" (Galatians 2:20).

In Colossians 3:3–4, the apostle wrote, "For you died, and your life is hidden with Christ in God. When Christ who is our life appears, then you also will appear with Him in glory." The Cross is the great test as regards life, for it is only those who come there and receive Christ by faith that have that new life. There is no life acceptable to God save in Christ and through Him. It is by the application of the truth of death that the believer knows the power of that life in experience. That is what is meant in 2 Corinthians 4:10–11, "Always carrying about in the body the dying of the Lord Jesus, that the life of Jesus also may be manifested in our body [mortal flesh]." The Cross in that way commits the believer to newness of life and newness of walk in the power of the Spirit. The flesh and the powers of the flesh must be mortified day by day if the new life is to be lived and enjoyed.

When the sons of Aaron were consecrated, the blood was first applied, and then they were anointed with oil. So believers must first know the power of the blood before the Holy Spirit can manifest His power in the life. The greater the place given to the Cross, the more will the power of the Spirit be manifested in the life.

SECRET OF TRUE SERVICE

"He died for all, that those who live should live no longer for themselves, but for Him who died for them and rose again" (2 Corinthians 5:15). In the previous verse, the great motive for true service is given in the words "For the love of Christ compels us." All true and acceptable service springs from the Cross, finding there its motive and its strength. There is only one place where Christ is spoken of as a bondservant (Philippians 2:7). In that passage, it tells of His emptying Himself and coming down from the glory to die on the cross of Calvary; and there He is set forth as the great example of the true servant, showing that service of any real effect calls for humility.

If the light is to shine forth with brilliancy, the earthen vessel must be broken, as in the case of Gideon's empty pitchers containing the lamps; then the excellency of the power is seen to be of God. "Not by might nor by power, but by My Spirit, says the Lord of hosts" (Zechariah 4:6). The great apostle to the Gentiles wrote to the Corinthians of his coming to them in weakness and fear and trembling, so that his testimony should not be in the wisdom of man, but in the demonstration and power of God. He gloried in infirmities, that the power of God might rest upon him, and in his weakness, that he might realize the power of God. In this way the Cross tests the servant in his service for God. It shows the great secret of effective service to be in turning away from all dependence on the flesh and putting complete trust in the Spirit of God, being obedient to Him. If service is to count, it must spring from love to Christ and be a work of faith.

When the risen Lord appeared to the disciples at the seaside, He drew forth from the apostle Peter the confession of his love and then commissioned him to feed and tend His sheep and lambs (John 21:15–17). It is a vision of Christ on the cross, and then the revelation of Him as the risen Lord, that appeals to the heart and produces devotion that finds expression in service.

Not only is the Cross the motive for service, but it is also the great message committed to every true servant of God. The message of the Cross is the one that appeals to all hearts and moves them to believe in Christ as Savior and yield to Him as Lord. Those who have learned its power in their own lives are able to tell it forth in its sweetness and fullness, so that it will appeal to the poor and needy among men and women. As the message of the Cross is sounded forth by those

whose hearts have been melted by it and who therefore know its power and blessedness in saving and
comforting, service will be rendered that will prove effective, find acceptance with God, and bring reward in
the Day of Judgment.

Doctrine, devotion, and duty find their motive at
the Cross, where all sufficiency is received for faithfulness and zeal, whether in daily living or in faithful service. The glory of God is the one supreme test of all
living and working, and it is at the Cross of Christ that
the glory of God shines out in all its brilliancy and
splendor. The measure in which the Cross is given
prominence in the life of the believer will determine
the measure in which God is glorified in that life and
its service.

CHAPTER THIRTEEN

THE TYPES OF
THE CROSS

*T*O GRASP THE FULL SIGNIFICANCE of the sacrifice and offering of Christ as taught in the epistle to the Hebrews, we need to look back to the Old Testament—to the teaching of types in Leviticus and other Old Testament books. In those books, the work of the Cross is pictured.

From the very beginning, after sin entered into the world, God required a sacrifice on the part of anyone who approached Him in worship or for blessing. That was why Abel's sacrifice was accepted and that of Cain refused; for the former was a slain animal speaking of death, whereas Cain's offering was that of his own hands. When the student comes to the history of Israel, he finds that their life as a nation began with the sprinkling of blood on the doorposts, giving safety from judgment by redemption; and that through all their life, sacrifice and offering held a large place. Their whole relationship with God and their preservation as a people depended on the constant offering up of sacrifices, for they had to be made daily, weekly, monthly, and yearly. As Paul later explained, "Now all these things happened to them as examples [types], and they were written for our admonition, upon whom the ends of the ages have come" (1 Corinthians 10:11).

The book of Leviticus teaches how a sinful person may approach God and then how one may walk with Him in communion, finding constant acceptance. God's provision was by sacrifice and priesthood, for it was only by acceptable sacrifice that anyone could come into the presence of God; and then his position there was maintained by the priest acting on his behalf.

The book opens therefore with the five great offerings, which present typically the person and work of Christ, the one perfect sacrifice. Three of these offerings were sweet savor offerings, and the other two were nonsweet savor offerings; in the first three the thought of sin is not prominent, as it is in the sin offering and the trespass offering. The sweet savor offering was one of rest or satisfaction to God, while the burnt offering, the meal offering, and the peace offering show how Christ offered Himself as a sacrifice to God, so as to please and delight Him and to fulfill His will.

WHY FIVE TYPICAL OFFERINGS?

The order in which these offerings are given is important, as well as the number of them; for "five" is a number particularly relating to mankind. "Five" points to responsibility and appropriation. This is shown in that every person has five fingers, five toes, and five senses. In the case of the hands and feet, these are doubled and indicate fullness of responsibility. In each of the offerings there are details in the instructions that point in some particular way to some aspect of the work of Christ or to some perfection in His person. They do not begin with the offering which meets man as a guilty sinner, but with the burnt offering, or the ascending offering, which went up to God for His delight and acceptance. The burnt offering not only had the first place, but it gave the name to the brazen altar where all sacrifices were offered, showing it to be the basal offering of all, the one which gave value to all the others. That is the offering which finds its fulfillment in Hebrews 10:7–10 and of which Psalm 40 speaks.

In the opening words of Leviticus, God declared through Moses that if anyone desired to come near to Him with an offering or an oblation, it must be a burnt sacrifice. It was to be of his own voluntary will and offered at the door of the tabernacle before the Lord. The offerer brought up his animal and presented it before the priest, laying his hand on its head; then it was slain and all of it was burnt on the altar. The word *burn*, when applied to what was put on the altar, means to go up or ascend, as the incense when burnt ascended as a fragrant smell from the golden altar. When anything was burnt outside the camp an entirely different word is used, meaning simply to consume or destroy.

All that was laid on the altar was for God and so ascended to Him for His acceptance. And so Christ offered Himself on the cross without spot to God for His delight and for His acceptance. As every offering had to be wholly without blemish, even so Christ offered Himself wholly to God.

ACCEPTANCE AND SATISFACTION

In the case of the burnt offering, all of the animal was burnt on the altar, but that was not so in the peace offering or any other sacrifices. The expression "of his own free will" means "for his acceptance," for that is one of the prominent ideas in the burnt offering. In going to the cross, Christ gave Himself an offering to God in order to delight the heart of God and to fulfill His will. He gave His whole being up to God for the satisfaction of His heart. In the burnt offering we foresee Christ presenting Himself in all His perfections to the Father; He was an offering that found perfect acceptance with God.

In the burnt offering the perfect will of God was fulfilled, for it was the fulfilling of God's eternal purpose, determined even before the creation of the world.

It presents an aspect of the Cross of Christ which is beyond the comprehension of man, for it did not have man's need in view so much as that which would please God and glorify Him. God ever saw in Christ perfections and beauties that were hidden from man, but that will be revealed in the coming glory.

The burnt offering presents to the believer that acceptance with God and satisfaction to God which is his in Christ, for by it he is sanctified and perfected forever (Hebrews 10:12–14). Though atonement was not permanent, every sacrifice on the altar had that in view, and it *is* said, "It will be accepted on his behalf to make atonement for him" (Leviticus 1:4). Later on, the idea of continuance is connected with the burnt offering (Numbers 28:6). That is the thought in the word "forever" in Hebrews 10:12–14, the meaning being "continually effective." The offering was made morning and evening by the priests, signifying continual acceptance.

CHRIST'S PERFECT OFFERING

The perfect offering of Christ, therefore, gives every believer perfect acceptance with God continually and eternally. It has made it possible for everyone coming to God to dwell in His presence; and not only so, but it gives everyone a place of delight before God. The one responsibility resting on the offerer was to lay his hand on the head of the sacrifice, showing his appropriation of it and his identification with it. The expression, "lay his hand" means lean his weight, signifying that all responsibility was put on the offering and borne by it. That finds its fulfillment in the acceptance by faith of Christ as Savior, and therefore everything that the one, perfect sacrifice of Christ accomplished was for the one who comes to Him by faith.

It is by the burnt offering that the believer is sanctified or made sacred to God, and also perfected before God forever; and it is the great incentive to believers to approach God with boldness at all times. Therefore, Paul wrote, "Let us draw near . . . in full assurance of faith" (Hebrews 10:22) and with boldness or liberty—with all fear gone forever. There is deep significance in the different animals provided for burnt offerings, but these will not be dealt with here.

THE GRAIN OFFERING

The second offering, recorded in the second chapter of Leviticus, is the grain, or meal, offering. It was a bloodless offering made of fine flour, with oil poured upon it and with frankincense put upon it. It was always associated with some other offerings, such as the burnt offering. A handful of the flour was burnt on the altar as a memorial, and the rest given to Aaron and his sons. The fine flour was earth's most precious product, providing food for man, and typifies Christ as the perfect man. It is His perfect life on earth as a man that is shown forth. As the fine flour was smooth and free from all grit or roughness, so the life of Christ as a man was perfectly even and free from all irritation, with never a ruffle whatever.

Though despised and rejected, misunderstood and misjudged, and treated with contempt and scorn by men, Jesus Christ was always perfectly righteous and even, loving even His enemies and seeking to do good to all He met. And not only was there the freedom from all that was uneven, but every grace had its perfect place and found perfect expression in His life. There were a perfectly even balance, and every virtue and grace was manifested constantly. No one trait of character predominated. He could truly say, "I do always those things that please him" (John 8:29).

Indeed, there was never a moment during His whole life, from His virgin birth into the world until He went to the cross, that His life was not perfectly pleasing to God and a delight to Him. God could look down every moment of His life and behold with satisfaction a man who was absolutely obeying His will and living every moment with the one object of pleasing and glorifying Him. At the close of His life, Jesus could say, "I have glorified You on the earth" (John 17:4).

The oil poured on the meal and also mingled with it, typifies the place and work of the Holy Spirit in the life of Christ; for oil is ever the type of the Spirit. The Son of Man was conceived and born of the Spirit of God. When He entered His work at His baptism, the Spirit descended as a dove upon Him. All of His works were wrought by the power of the Spirit. Throughout

His whole life He spoke and worked in perfect dependence upon the Spirit of God. When He went to the cross, He offered Himself through the eternal Spirit, and it was by the power of the Spirit that He was raised from among the dead.

A handful of frankincense was a memorial on the altar. A fragrant spice and perfectly white, the frankincense spoke of the fragrance of Christ's spotless life to God. The Savior's life was one of love and devotion, which found all its delight and satisfaction in pleasing God and showing forth who the Father is. As a memorial, the frankincense would point to that perfect life, ever to be kept in remembrance—for after His resurrection, Christ ascended to the right hand of God and is there today as a glorified man.

THE INCARNATION OF CHRIST NECESSARY

God's purpose for Adam in his creation was thwarted by Adam's fall in the Garden, but Christ as the perfect man came to redeem the whole race and become the federal head of a new creation. The new man, formed in Christ, the head, and of the church, the body, will have his place with God eternally through the work of the Son of Man, Christ Jesus.

The incarnation of Christ was an absolute necessity; everything connected with it was essential. He had to come into the world virgin-born, or He could not fulfill the purpose of God and bring to man that redemption called for on account of sin. In His incarnation, all that was brought about was absolutely perfect and perfectly in accord with the will of God. All that He as a man accomplished counts for man and will find its full fruition when all created things will be made subject to man, as pictured in Psalm 8 and Hebrews 2.

THE PEACE OFFERING

These two offerings and the peace offering were the sweet savor offerings, the peace offering being described in the third chapter of Leviticus. The peace offering differed from the burnt offering in that only part of it was put on the altar, as both the priest and the offerer received some part of the animal sacrificed. In that respect it differed from all other offerings. As in all sacrifices, the offering had to be without blemish and without spot, meaning that it could have no defect whatever nor be tainted in any way. Thus it would typify truly the Lamb of God, the one perfect sacrifice in the sight of God.

In the peace offering, the fat of the animal was burnt on the altar and the blood was sprinkled round about the altar. The word "fat" is rendered in other places as "best," and it represents the energy of life, pointing again to that which Christ offered to God when He gave Himself on the cross. It was taken from the internal parts and the kidneys; that speaks of the inward devotion of Christ's life and the centering of all of His love and desires and longings in the will of God and in pleasing Him.

EFFICACY OF THE BLOOD

The blood spoke of a life sacrificed, for God required death if sin was to be put away and if anyone was to approach Him. "The life of the flesh is in the blood" (Leviticus 17:11). That, however, always points to the life poured out to death, and not as the blood flowing through the veins and arteries in life, as some are teaching. The blood was put on the horns of the altar, and poured round about it, witnessing to the life having been sacrificed. The Lamb seen in glory will be "as though it had been slain" (Revelation 5:6). It will be through the blood of the Lamb that the redeemed will have their place around the throne of God and the Lamb.

The word *peace* in both Old and New Testaments means wholeness or fullness, and therefore oneness. The peace offering brought the offerer into oneness with God, which meant reconciliation, for by it all that caused separation was put away. *Reconciliation* means the removal of strife, or contention, or enmity, and so the bringing together as friends those who previously had enmity. That friendship finds its expression in fellowship or communion. That was the meaning when the offerer, the priest, and God all shared in the offering and took part of it as food. Eating together is the way in which fellowship is expressed throughout the Scriptures.

The peace offering was a praise or thank offering.

Hence, we are to "continually offer the sacrifice of praise to God, that is, the fruit of our lips giving thanks [confession] to His name" (Hebrews 13:15).

By the Cross of Christ, as the peace offering, the believer is brought into oneness with God, being at peace with Him, for He "made peace through the blood of His cross" (Colossians 1:20). By the peace offering, He broke down the wall of partition between Jew and Gentile and made them one in Christ. All enmity, strife, and contention are done away at the Cross of Christ, and all who come there in faith are made one in Christ; and so all believers are brought into fellowship with one another, as well as with Him. Whatever, therefore, divides believers and hinders their communion is not of the Cross but rather nullifies its place and power. Believers are "called into the fellowship of His Son, Jesus Christ our Lord"; and they are all members of His body, being "one bread and one body" (1 Corinthians 1:9; 10:17).

THE SIN OFFERING

The two nonsweet savor offerings were the sin and trespass offerings. Much greater space in Leviticus is given to these two offerings than to the other three. While in the first three chapters of Leviticus fifty-one verses are devoted to the sweet savor offerings, sixty-one verses in chapters four, five, and six describe the sin and trespass offerings.

The names of these offerings indicate that they are

connected particularly with sin, and therefore atoning in their effect. Also there are very real differences in these two offerings; for *trespass* means guilt or wrong done, while *sin* includes all failure and shortcoming. The trespass offering was for wrong, injury, or harm done by the sinner; but the sin offering atoned for the sinner and his sinfulness, as well as securing forgiveness for sins committed. The offerings in both cases needed to be whole and without defect, otherwise they could not atone for sin. In their perfections, they pointed to Him who is sinless, "Him who knew no sin" (2 Corinthians 5:21).

In the sin offering, provision was made for the priest who sinned, for a ruler, for the whole congregation, and for anyone of the common people. In each case there was some difference in the ritual, but the main points were similar. In every instance, even if one had sinned through ignorance or unwittingly, when his sin was known, the offering had to be brought to the tabernacle of the congregation. Sin is sin whether the sinner knows of its committal or not; nor does God ever pass over sin but requires for every sin the necessary sacrifice. It is only by death that sin can be atoned for and only on the ground of sacrifice that it can be forgiven.

When the animal was brought to the altar and killed, the priest took its blood and put it on the horns of the altar and sprinkled it round about the altar or at the bottom of it. The fat of the animal was burnt on the altar, and the carcass was taken outside the camp and there consumed. When all that was required was done, it is said that "the priest shall make atonement for them, and it shall be forgiven them" (Leviticus 4:20).

For a priest, or the whole congregation, the offering had to be a young bull, but a ruler or one of the common people might bring a kid of the goats, or a lamb, or two pigeons, or even a meal offering. That surely indicates that God would bring the offering within reach of the poorest, so that none might have any excuse for not making an offering. Seeing that a grain offering would provide an atonement, where there was no sacrifice, nor blood shed, it may be thought that where there is recognition of the person of Christ as Savior, apart from knowledge of all that His death on the cross means, God will forgive the sinner. But it is on the ground of the blood atonement made, and because of what God sees in Christ and in His finished work, that He can justly forgive sin. That would not apply where the blood as an atonement for sin is rejected or the Cross of Christ despised. There surely have been weak souls who have believed in Jesus Christ as Savior and have loved Him truly, and yet they have had little or no knowledge of the doctrine connected with His work on the Cross or the meaning of His shed blood.

In the sweet savor offerings, the offerer had to lay his hand upon the head of the offering, signifying his appropriation of it and his identification with it. That act also meant the acknowledgment of his sin and consequent need; for the one essential condition required for forgiveness is confession of the sin committed. That is the great truth in Psalm 32, where the psalmist shows that so long as his sin was unconfessed he had no peace or rest. However, "if we confess our sins, He is faithful and just to forgive us our sins and to cleanse us from all unrighteousness" (1 John 1:9).

All that the sacrifice of Christ on the cross meant as regards sin counts for the believer. His death was the complete and final answer to all sin, and everyone coming to Christ and accepting Him as Savior and Lord is forgiven all sin and fully cleared. The question of sin is answered for them. "He was wounded for our transgressions . . . and by His stripes we are healed" (Isaiah 53:5).

THE TRESPASS OFFERING

In the case of the trespass offering, it was always a ram that had to be sacrificed, and that offering spoke of value or worth. It was offered also when the priests were consecrated to their service for God. Acts of trespass or wrongdoing might be in the holy things, such as worship or service for God, and also in one's relationship with others. In the former it might be a matter of ignorance, but not when dealing with a neighbor. In the sin offering, the sinner saw his sin dealt with and what he was as a sinner, but in the trespass offering, it is what he had done. In the case of a trespass, the priest had to estimate the value of it and payment had to be made as recompense or restitution. That estimation had to be made by the priest, for no sinner can truly estimate the awfulness of the wrong done by his offense. It is God alone who can judge what sin means and what it deserves.

The word "trespass" is the word "offense," used of the fall of Adam in Romans 5 (vv. 15–16, 20). The heinousness of man's trespass was such that it demanded the awful sufferings endured by the Son of God on the cross; and it is there that we learn how God estimates man's offense and what the Fall meant.

Man's standards, however high, fall far short of those of a perfectly righteous and holy God, who cannot look upon sin or iniquity except with abhorrence. By man's trespass both God and man have been wronged, and restitution must be made for the injury done. By the offering of Christ, God will get His rights which were infringed by the Fall, and man also will receive rights even more than he lost. That is what is shown by the addition of the fifth part to the estimation by the priest.

The import of that fifth part is explained by its first occurrence in the Bible (Genesis 47:18–26), where it was appointed by Joseph as the amount to be paid to Pharaoh by the people who had forfeited their land and were absolutely dependent on the bounty of Pharaoh for all their living. That payment was the recognition by them that they belonged to Pharaoh and owed to him all that they were and had. They were his people, but now they belonged to him in a new way, for through the famine they had lost all, and but for grace shown by him would have perished. It is therefore a witness to God's grace in connection with the work of Christ on the Cross that helps to explain the "much more" of Romans 5.

BY BETTER SACRIFICES

Christ not only gave Himself as a guilt offering and put away man's sin and cleared the sinner of judgment and condemnation, but He brought to the believer far more than he ever could have had, even though He had not sinned. If Adam had maintained his innocence, he would have had a creature righteousness and been abundantly blessed on the earth; but those who have sinned and now believe on Christ as Savior and Lord and are saved by His sacrifice, receive the righteousness of God and become heirs of God and joint heirs with Christ. Moreover, they have the blessed hope of the coming glory in the presence of God eternally—blessings that Adam never could have known.

By the Cross of Christ the believer is brought to such a place of blessing and security that it is impossible for him ever to lose or forfeit it; for he is God's new creation and made one with God in Christ and destined to eternal glory. And not only so, but God will receive far greater glory through the sacrifice of Christ as the trespass offering than He would have received if sin had not entered into the world. That is what the addition of the fifth part in the trespass offering signifies. "Where sin abounded, grace abounded much more " (Romans 5:20). When the teaching of Romans 3 and 5 is studied in the light of these points in the trespass offering, the fullness of the work of Christ on the cross and the wonders of that offering shine out with greater splendor than otherwise possible: "That as sin reigned in death, even so grace might reign through righteousness to eternal life through Jesus Christ our Lord" (Romans 5:21).

CHAPTER FOURTEEN

THE BLOOD OF CHRIST

THE DEATH OF CHRIST AT CALVARY is a fact of history and therefore does not call for more than ordinary intelligence to be accepted. It is different, however, with the blood of Christ, for that involves theological truth and therefore appeals to faith. When one understands the meaning of the blood of Christ, it signifies that he has accepted Christ as a personal Savior and has believed the Word of God unto salvation. To speak, therefore, of the blood of Christ is to appeal to faith and not to mere reason or knowledge.

If one is to use Scripture accurately, he must admit that redemption is not by the death of Christ but by His blood, for that is its meaning in the New Testament (Romans

3:24–25; Ephesians 1:7; 1 Peter 1:18–19). The blood includes death, for it points back to the types in the Old Testament and to the sacrifices offered on the altar, and implies the believer's appropriation of the truth therein revealed.

The first reference to blood is in Genesis 4:10–11, where the blood of Abel is spoken of as crying out from the ground for vengeance. It is contrasted with the blood of Christ in Hebrews 12:24, for His blood cries out for mercy and blessing, even to His enemies. Blood therefore speaks of a life taken or slain. "For the life of the flesh is in the blood, and I have given it to you upon the altar to make an atonement for your souls; for it is the blood that makes atonement for the soul" (Leviticus 17:11). This is further borne out by the next reference, in Genesis 9:4–6, where the shedding of man's blood is required by God of him who shed it. So throughout the whole of the Old Testament, references to the blood point to death and responsibility with regard to it. There are very many passages in which blood is mentioned as connected with the death of people, but we are now dealing with the word as it is connected with the Cross of Christ, the blood of sacrifice.

The various references to the blood of Christ in the New Testament show that it is connected with every part of the Christian life, from its very inception to its final consummation in glory. This is indicated by the way in which the blood of the sacrifices is emphasized in the Old Testament. The great foundation passage is Exodus 12, where the blood of the paschal lamb was appointed to be put upon the lintel and the doorposts of each house on the night the destroying angel passed through the land, and by means of which the people found deliverance from death. That was the night of the redemption of Israel from their bondage in Egypt; and it was the blood that secured their safety from judgment. For God had said, "When I see the blood, I will pass over you; and the plague shall not be on you to destroy you when I strike the land of Egypt" (Exodus 12:13). The death of the firstborn was the last of the ten judgments upon Egypt, directed against Pharaoh and his people, to make them willing to let His people go.

GOD'S PASSOVER PROVIDED

The instructions to the people of Israel through Moses were that they should take a lamb for each household, that it should be kept apart for four days and then slain and its blood put upon the lintel and the two doorposts. It was to be a token or sign that there had been death by sacrifice, so that when God saw it, He would pass over the door and not allow the destroyer to enter. In every house where there was no blood, the angel entered, and the death of the firstborn was the result. "And it came to pass at midnight that the Lord struck all the firstborn in the land of Egypt, from the firstborn of Pharaoh who sat on his throne to the firstborn of the captive who was in the dungeon, and all the firstborn of livestock" (Exodus 12: 29).

When the lamb was slain, a bunch of hyssop was dipped into the blood in the basin and struck on the lintel and two side posts of the door. As a common weed, hyssop speaks of the faith that is common to all of God's people. The words "pass over" referring to God's protection of the people is not the word for "pass by" or "pass through," as the crossing of a river, or passing through a town or country. It occurs as "pass over" in Exodus 12:13, 23, 27, and is found in four other places, as follows: 2 Samuel 4:4; 1 Kings 18:21 (KJV), "halt"; 26, "leaped", "became lame"; Isaiah 31:5, "passing over." It means passing over from one foot to the other, or hovering over; and that meant that God stood over the houses and so came between His people and the destroying angel. He became their safety.

The Feast of the Passover received its name from that historical fact and was commemorated yearly. The word "sprinkle" does not occur in Exodus 12:22; it is the word "strike" that is used, frequently rendered "touch" or "reach to." In Hebrews 11, however, it is said of Moses that "by faith he kept the Passover and the sprinkling of blood" (v. 28). The act of putting the blood on the doorposts indicated faith in the word of God. It was the blood of redemption, securing Israel's safety from judgment and making them the people of God by purchase.

In Romans 3, where man is shown to be a guilty sinner, having no righteousness of his own, it is on the ground of the blood of redemption that he is justified by faith (see vv. 24–25). In Romans 5:9 the believer is said to be "justified by His blood." That chapter emphasizes the security of the believer and the permanence of his position as justified; for it is by blood and not by faith, though the great truth of that epistle is justification by faith. Then in Ephesians it is declared, "We have redemption through His blood, the forgiveness of sins, according to the riches of His grace" (Ephesians 1:7); and almost the same words are repeated in Colossians 1:14.

ACCESS BY THE BLOOD

It is the blood of Christ that is the sole ground of forgiveness and our acceptance by God. "Without shedding of blood there is no remission" (Hebrews 9:22). Hebrews corresponds with Leviticus, where the truth of access to God by sacrifice is revealed, and a walk with God in sanctification is maintained by a God-appointed priesthood. In Romans 5, Colossians 1, and Ephesians 2, the believer is shown to have peace with God, being reconciled and having access into His presence through the blood; from Hebrews 10:19–20 we learn that the way into the Holiest is by the blood, which gives boldness.

No sinner could approach God in his sin, but by the blood of Christ forgiveness and cleansing is secured;

and when accepted by faith, that cleansed sinner has access with boldness into the very Holy of Holies. That was something quite unknown and utterly impossible to any Israelite, for until the veil was rent, the way into God's presence in the Holy of Holies was closed. It was when the blood of Christ was shed on the cross that God Himself rent the veil and opened the way for all who would come by faith in Christ.

The action of the high priest in going into the Holiest on the great Day of Atonement once a year with the blood of the sin offering, which he sprinkled on and before the mercy seat, typified the action of Christ when He ascended to the right hand of God. As the high priest acted as a representative, so does Christ, and where He is, the believer may come by faith, that is, to the throne of grace with boldness. It is the blood of Christ that gives the believer this boldness.

The next reference to the blood in Exodus is in chapter twenty-four (vv. 6, 8), where the blood of the covenant was sprinkled by Moses, first on the altar and then on the people. Following upon that act, Moses together with Aaron and the elders of the people went up into the mount to meet God. That incident (mentioned in Hebrews 9:19–23) connects the blood of the covenant with the remission of sins as necessary for any communion with God.

There are just three references to the blood of Christ in the Synoptic Gospels (Matthew 26:28; Mark

14:24; Luke 22:20), all of them being the words of Christ when instituting the Lord's Supper on the night of His betrayal. He spoke of His blood as the blood of the new covenant and of its being shed for the remission of sins. It is the blood therefore that is the basis of all covenant relationship with God, and by it alone can one find access into His holy presence and enjoy communion with Him.

THE ABRAHAMIC COVENANT

The word *covenant* in the New Testament is formed by two words meaning to come together. It therefore describes a mutual agreement or undertaking entered into by two parties by which they bind themselves to fulfill certain obligations. The Greek word, however, it is said, does not in itself contain the idea of a joint agreement but rather an obligation undertaken by one person towards another or others. That was certainly the meaning of the covenant made with Abraham, for God alone was responsible for the fulfillment of its promised blessing. The only responsibility resting on Abraham was that of faith.

And that is the covenant according to which believers are blessed now, according to Galatians 3. It is a covenant requiring of us only faith. This covenant is called to mind when believers gather to remember the Lord in the breaking of bread and thus show forth His death till He returns. The blood of Christ pledges God to fulfill all that is promised in the covenant with

His people in Christ, and that is done wherever faith accepts it by accepting Christ.

The only mention of the blood in Acts refers to the blood as the purchase price paid for the church of God (Acts 20:28). It is the purchase by blood that makes any church, for every true church of God is formed of redeemed people; and only those who are redeemed by the blood of Christ can truly call themselves the church of God. Every church of God is a flock of God's people to be shepherded by overseers made such by the Holy Spirit. Wherever the expression "church of God" occurs, it will be found to refer to a local assembly, gathering in the name of the Lord, and not to the whole body of believers, called "the church" in fourteen places.

It is in the book of Leviticus that the greatest prominence is given to this teaching about the blood, for it records the great body of laws given to the people of Israel when they were brought out of Egypt into the wilderness; and these laws taught them how a holy God could dwell among a sinful people and how they might walk with Him in blessed communion and enjoy His guidance and protection. The way of access into His presence was by sacrifice; and the walk with Him was maintained by their separation from evil and by the ministry of the priesthood. These are the two great truths of Hebrews which explain the typical teaching of Leviticus.

The five great offerings and their significance have

been mentioned in the previous chapter. Leviticus 16 and 17 are key chapters, describing the yearly Day of Atonement and the significance of the blood. The tenth day of the seventh month was the great day each year in the life of Israel as a nation. That was the one day in the year when the high priest went into the Holy of Holies, carrying a basin of blood from the sin offering and sprinkling it on the mercy seat and before it, witnessing to God of the offering which had been made as an atonement for sin. That act had to be repeated year by year, showing that sin was not put away and no perfection was obtained by what was done then.

THE BLOOD OF CHRIST

Hebrews 9–10 contrasts the one offering of Christ and His ministry as High Priest with the Old Testament ceremonies. This portion of Scripture teaches that Christ perfected the way into the Holiest and also made perfect those who approach by His blood, perfect as far as the conscience is concerned. His one perfect offering for sin and His entrance into the Holy of Holies has procured for every believer a purged conscience and has made it possible for every one to approach God directly in the Holiest and be maintained there constantly. The whole emphasis in Hebrews 9 is the blood of Christ. His blood has obtained eternal redemption; it has purged the conscience; it has secured for us an eternal inheritance; and it is the blood of the covenant.

The blood was invariably put upon the altar or the mercy seat and not upon the persons, except in the case of the blood of the covenant, or when it was put on the leper at the time of his cleansing or on the priest at the time of his consecration. It is important to recognize this when examining passages on cleansing from sin, as in 1 John 1:7: "The blood of Jesus Christ His Son cleanses us from all sin." That word is addressed to believers who walk in the light, as a word of encouragement; for if one walks in the light it should make him realize his unworthiness. Thus God reminds all such that it is the blood of Jesus that gives them a place in His presence and keeps them there. The cleansing is from all sin, not sins; and so the verses which follow teach of the provision for the cleansing from acts of sin by the advocacy of Christ and by the confession of the one who has sinned. The blood clears the believer before God, for it has made atonement for his sin and has brought him into God's holy presence with perfect acceptance.

There is no scriptural warrant for the idea of washing the believer in *blood*; for personal cleansing was by washing in *water*. The very first act in the consecration of the priest was his being bathed in water, and that was followed by the offerings for sin and by the anointing with oil. When the leper was clean and ready to be restored to the camp (Leviticus 14), the priest took the two birds provided, killed one and then dipped the living one in the blood of the other, and

sprinkled the leper seven times, after which the leper
was bathed and brought into the camp. He had to provide certain offerings, and the priest took the blood of
the trespass offering in his left hand and with his right
finger put some on the tip of his right ear, on the
thumb of his right hand, and on the great toe of his
right foot. That marked these parts by death, and so
signified their separation from sin and unto God. They
are the extremities of man, and thus his whole being
was separated by death. The ear was to hear the voice
of God; the hand was for service and for fellowship
with others; and the foot spoke of the walk or personal
conduct—all being marked by death as that which put
away sin.

In the consecration of the priests, they were first
bathed, then clothed; then the sin offering and the
burnt offering were sacrificed, and the priests laid
their hands on them. That was followed by the ram of
consecration being offered, and it was the blood of
that offering that was put upon their right ears,
thumbs, and toes. Then, having filled their hands with
the parts of the offerings to be waved before the Lord,
Moses took oil and blood and sprinkled them and
their garments, and so sanctified them.

The order followed in these Levitical ceremonies
was that the blood came first and then the oil; for it is
only where the blood of the sacrifice is recognized as
the basis of blessing that the oil representing the Holy
Spirit is received. The consecration of the priests by

blood points to the sanctification by blood taught in Hebrews. Every one believing in Christ is sanctified by God (Hebrews 10:10), for sanctification means to set apart or make sacred that which belongs to God. The sanctification made by the sacrifices under the law was an outward one and applied to the flesh; whereas that made by the blood of Christ means a purged conscience and an inward sanctification. Hence, we have the exhortation in Hebrews 12:14, "Pursue peace with all people, and holiness, without which no one will see the Lord." That is the holiness secured by the blood of Christ, in contrast with the sanctification provided by the Levitical offerings. The Hebrews were in danger of being satisfied with their legal sacrifices, and the ceremonies connected with the temple and the priesthood, and of turning away from Christ and His perfect sacrifice and priesthood.

There is little doubt but that the true rendition of Revelation 1:5 is "To Him who loved us and washed us from our sins in His own blood." There is a reference in Revelation 7:14 to the washing of robes and making them white in the blood of the Lamb by those who come out of the Great Tribulation, but that company is not the church of this age. Robes represent "righteous acts" as we learn from Revelation 19:8, but the righteousness of the saints is the very righteousness of God, which can never be sullied and requires no washing. A better rendering, too, would be *by* the blood of the Lamb, instead of *in* the blood of the Lamb. It is in line with the victory achieved over Satan in Revelation 12:11.

WASHING OF REGENERATION

Cleansing by water is frequently mentioned in Scripture, and, as has been noticed, was the first act in the consecration of the priests. It points to regeneration, or the new birth (Titus 3:5). Hence our Lord said, when washing the feet of the disciples on the night of His betrayal, "He who is bathed needs only to wash his feet, but is completely clean" (John 13:10); and so in other passages where washing by water is referred to (John 15:3; Ephesians 5:26). The washing in 1 Corinthians 6:11 evidently refers to the washing of the priests at their consecration, for it is followed by "sanctified" and "justified." The sanctifying is the setting apart, or making sacred; the justifying includes the acts of faith which give evidence of their position as believers and their ministry as priests.

In the tabernacle, the brazen altar stood at the door of the court and was the first place to which anyone came in approaching God. From there he went to the laver, where the hands and feet were washed in water before he entered into the holy place. So in Hebrews 10:22, we are exhorted to draw near with full assurance of faith, having our hearts sprinkled from an evil conscience, which was done at the laver. It is the blood that cleanses from the guilt and defilement of sin; and the Word of God used by the Spirit of God cleanses from the power of sin (Psalm 119:9).

There is also the twofold truth of redemption by the blood, which purges the conscience, and the cleansing by water, which points to regeneration by the Word. Everything connected with the priestly ministry was on the basis of the shedding of blood at the altar, and then the cleansing at the laver. That was the only way of approach to God and the only ground on which any service could be rendered to Him. And so all worship and all service now is made acceptable through the better sacrifices offered at Calvary. That is what is meant in Hebrews 9:23 by "the heavenly things themselves" being purified by better sacrifices than the Old Testament sacrifices. Servants of God are apt to take satisfaction in their service for God because of the earnestness and devotion they put into it. Again, others are sometimes discouraged because they feel that they come so far short. Then often those who are the most devoted and zealous are the most discouraged. While none can ever render too devoted or earnest service, it must be recognized that everything that is done in faith is purified and made acceptable by the blood and by the high-priestly ministry of the Lord Jesus.

THE LORD'S TABLE

God gave to Israel very solemn prohibitions against eating the fat or drinking the blood of the sacrifices, and anyone doing so was in danger of being cut off from among the people. But the Lord Jesus said,

"Unless you eat the flesh of the Son of Man and drink His blood, you have no life in you" (John 6:53); and "Whoever eats My flesh and drinks My blood has eternal life"; and again, "He who eats My flesh and drinks My blood abides in Me, and I in him" (John 6:54, 56). He was the bread of life coming down from heaven. By eating and drinking He meant receiving by faith the gift of life, as He explained in John 7:37–38.

Those words in John 6 do not refer to eating and drinking the bread and wine at the Lord's Supper, for that is not the ground of receiving eternal life. The gospel of John makes it very clear that eternal life is a gift received by believing on Christ according to the Word of God. The partaking of the bread and wine at the Lord's Table is an act of worship and expresses fellowship with Him and with those at the table. The bread and the wine are simply memorials of the body and blood of Christ. Believers do not come to the Lord's Table to feed on Christ but to take the emblems provided in memory of Him and of His death for them, recognizing that they have already eternal life by faith in Him as Savior and Lord.

As believers read and meditate daily upon the Word of God, they are directed to Christ and His work—they are feeding upon Him and so dwelling in Him. That is the one essential thing to maintain true life and to develop it. As the Word of God is neglected, there will surely be loss of blessing and failure to grow in grace.

Notice in 1 Corinthians 10:16–17 that the blood is put first, whereas in 1 Corinthians 11 the bread is mentioned first. The reason is that in chapter ten the Lord's Table and the fellowship of saints are in view; therefore the blood must be put first, for it is the sole ground on which anyone may come to His table in an acceptable way. In chapter eleven, the Lord's Supper is emphasized, and the Lord is given first place; therefore, the bread which speaks of His person is first. The chief thought is worship, recognizing His rightful place as Lord. The Lord's Table is therefore only for those who are saved through the merits of the blood of Christ, for it is only such who can truly take in their hands the bread and wine as memorials of His person and His death and give thanks for them.

MANY WITNESSES

"There are three that bear witness on earth: the Spirit, the water, and the blood; and these three agree as one" (1 John 5:8). In verse 6 we read, "This is He who came by water and blood—Jesus Christ; not only by water, but by water and blood." It was by water and blood, not by blood and water. John 19:34 records that when the soldier pierced His side, there came out blood and water; but in this passage in 1 John it is water and blood. In John's epistle there are different manifestations of Christ mentioned. In chapter one (v. 2), the life was manifested, pointing to His coming as a man; chapter three (v. 8) notes His manifestation at the

Cross; then chapters two (v. 28) and three (v. 2), tell of His future manifestation when He shall come again.

The two definitive events in the manifestation of Christ were His baptism and His death, so that He came by water and by blood. All three witnesses quoted above point to the one truth "that Jesus is the Son of God" (1 John 5:5). At the baptism of Jesus, the Father bore witness to Him as His beloved Son in the words "This is My beloved Son, in whom I am well pleased" (Matthew 3:17). By His death, Christ Himself witnessed that He was the Son of God, and then by the Scriptures. By His words and works, the Holy Spirit witnessed to Him as the Son of God. At least ten times in 1 John 5, Christ is mentioned as the Son and the Son of God. "He who has the Son has life; he who does not have the Son of God does not have life" (1 John 5:12).

The testimony of John at the close of his gospel is that it was written to prove "that Jesus is the Christ, the Son of God, and that believing you may have life in His name" (John 20:31). And in his first epistle, John tells of the threefold witness by the three persons of the Trinity to this great truth, which is the very foundation of all faith and life; for the greatest need of all men under sin and death is life—eternal life, and that life is in the Son of God.

In the Revelation of Jesus Christ, where future scenes of glory are described, the great host of the redeemed in heaven are ascribing glory and honor to

Christ as the slain Lamb, because He had redeemed them by His blood. They recognize that their presence in glory is due to the blood of the slain Lamb; and their voices unite in the cry, "Worthy is the Lamb who was slain to receive power and riches and wisdom and strength and honor and glory and blessing!" (Revelation 5:12). Everyone in heaven is there on the ground of the blood of the slain Lamb. Then the worth of the blood of the Lamb will be fully realized; hence the cry, "Worthy." Throughout the eternal ages it will be the blood of the Lamb that will give the redeemed their place in the presence of God and the Lamb.

"Knowing that you were not redeemed with corruptible things, like silver or gold, from your aimless conduct received by tradition from your fathers, but with the precious blood of Christ, as of a lamb without blemish and without spot" (I Peter 1:18–19).

When I survey the wondrous cross
On which the Prince of glory died,
My richest gain I count but loss,
And pour contempt on all my pride.

See, from His head, His hands, His feet,
Sorrow and love flow mingled down;
Did e'er such love and sorrow meet,
Or thorns compose so rich a crown?

Were the whole realm of nature mine,
That were a present far too small:
Love so amazing, so divine,
Demands my soul, my life, my all.
　　　　　　　—Isaac Watts

CHAPTER FIFTEEN

THE EXPLANATIONS
OF THE CROSS

MEN AND WOMEN CONSTANTLY ask questions regarding spiritual matters, and most of those center on the subjects of sin and its remedy, God's dealings with mankind, and the future state. Almost every such question will find an answer at the Cross of Christ, for it is there that the great mysteries of God and of Christ and of God's purposes for the world are explained by His word to the believer.

It must be acknowledged that God Himself is a wonderful mystery in His being, His character, and His ways of dealing with His people and with mankind. Then there are the mysteries about Christ as man and God, as well as His work of redemption. When the subject of sin and its consequences is raised, along with the destiny of the saved and the unsaved, there is no end to the difficulties that occur to inquirers. The death of Christ on the cross and His resurrection from among the dead have answered a host of questions that have troubled many before they came to know the Lord Jesus as a personal Savior. His death and resurrection also have given them a vision of God Himself and something of His wonderful purposes of wisdom and grace.

Until a sinner has come to recognize the exceeding sinfulness of his sin and has looked to Christ on the cross as the only Savior from that sin, there are questions on spiritual things that never can be solved. "The natural man does not receive the things of the Spirit of God, for they are foolishness to him; nor can he know them, because they are spiritually discerned" (1 Corinthians 2:14). One may have great intellectual ability, have had wonderful educational advantages, been trained theologically, and even engaged in religious work, and yet if that one has not been born again by the Spirit of God, he is in darkness regarding the things of God. But if he receives Christ as a personal Savior and is born of God, he obtains spiritual light and a knowledge of God and the things of God in a way otherwise impossible. "If anyone is in Christ, he is a new creation" (2 Corinthians 5:17), and no amount of explanation of spiritual things is of any value whatever until that change has been experienced.

At the same time, there are honest souls who are

willing to receive information that helps to meet their difficulties and so prepare them to take this step of faith. Wherever there are honest souls ready to be convinced of the truth of God and to walk in the light given, God will meet them and give further light and help. Our Lord laid down a great principle when He said, "If anyone wills to do His will, he shall know concerning the doctrine" (John 7:17).

REVELATION OF GOD NECESSARY

"God is a Spirit" (John 4:24 KJV) and therefore if He is to be known by man there must be a revelation of Himself; and that revelation is given in the Scriptures. He has also made Himself known in creation by His wonderful works, which are constantly witnessing to His wisdom and power. "Since the creation of the world His invisible attributes are clearly seen, being understood by the things that are made, even His eternal power and Godhead" (Romans 1:20).

The central point in the revelation of God by His Word is the Cross of Christ, for all of His works in creation lead up to that event; and everything was brought into being by Him for the display of His wisdom, power, and love in the giving of His only Son as the redeemer of the world.

"God is light and in Him is no darkness at all" (1 John 1:5). Light means knowledge; also holiness and righteousness. Nowhere are the holiness and righteousness of God seen so wonderfully as at the Cross of Christ, where His power was put forth to the very utmost in order to put away sin and defeat all the powers of darkness. In that way He manifested the perfection of His character as a holy God.

LOVE AT THE CROSS

"God is love" (1 John 4:8). Love is the very essence of His being, and all He does is in love. It is around this truth about God that so many questions rage. Skeptics say, "If He is a God of love, why is there so much misery in the world? Why is there a devil? Why are so many allowed to suffer?" Countless other questions could be propounded of a similar nature. There is only one place where these questions can find an answer, and that is at the Cross of Christ. "By this we know love, because He laid down His life for us . . . In this the love of God was manifested toward us, that God has sent His only begotten Son into the world, that we might live through Him. In this is love, not that we loved God, but that He loved us and sent His Son to be the propitiation for our sins" (1 John 3:16; 4:9–10). "For God so loved the world that He gave His only begotten Son, that whoever believes in Him should not perish but have everlasting life" (John 3:16).

The one great manifestation of the love of God for sinful men is the Cross of the Lord Jesus Christ, and since God in His great love for sinners and those who are His enemies gave up His own Son to that shameful and ignominious death on their behalf, there is no reason whatever for any question about His love; nor has any man the right for a moment to judge that love by circumstances or events, whatever they may be.

The deliverance of His Son to death was no afterthought with God, for it was His purpose for all eternity. Christ was the Lamb slain from before the foundation of the world. He was "delivered by the determined purpose and foreknowledge of God" (Acts 2:23). The death and the resurrection of Christ, according to the eternal plan of God, were for the redemption of sinners and for blessing to the whole world. The Cross of Christ is the very pivot around which revolves the whole plan of God for mankind. It reveals His perfect wisdom, the understanding of which will help to solve many of the problems connected with the evils of this present age. It is the failure to recognize God's plan as revealed in the Scriptures that causes so many questions to arise in the minds of men and women with regard to the happenings in this world and to question His love and wisdom.

A NEW PLAN

God has divided up time into different periods, and in each period He has dealt with man in a different way, conferring upon Him different privileges and putting on Him different responsibilities. For instance, when Adam was placed in the Garden of Eden, he had wonderful privileges of blessing but the one responsibility not to eat of a particular tree. When dealing with Noah and his family, God imposed conditions that were by no means similar. Then in the history of Abraham, God presented entirely different conditions and responsibilities.

In these different ages or periods, God made covenants with His people. There was one made with Noah, another with Abraham, and still others with Moses and David on behalf of Israel as the nation of God. According to these covenants, God's dealings with people differed during these periods. But by the death of Christ on the cross and His resurrection, mankind has been put on a different footing before God—for the Cross has made it possible for God to reach out to the guiltiest and vilest sinner and to offer freely to all a full salvation from all sin.

By the events at Calvary and Pentecost, a new era altogether has been introduced in which grace is reigning through righteousness. In this period, God is doing a new thing, never done before; for by the preaching of the Gospel and by the work of the Holy Spirit, He is gathering from among all nations a body of believers united to Christ, called the church. When that body is complete, God will send the Lord Jesus for all who belong to that body. At that moment, they will be changed into His likeness and be forever with Him. That will be followed by further dealings with Israel as a nation, and through that nation blessing will flow forth to the whole world.

Some knowledge of this wonderful purpose of God and its application to the present evil time will help to clear up many of the questions that arise regarding God and His ways with the world. A knowledge of that plan and God's ways and methods of carrying it out must impress upon everyone the perfection of it, calling forth wonder and praise, as well as being a rebuke to all unbelief. At the close of Romans 11, where the purpose of God for Israel particularly is unfolded, showing how that nation is yet to be blessed through the coming of the Deliverer out of Zion, is the doxology "Oh, the depth of the riches both of the wisdom and knowledge of God! How unsearchable are His judgments and His ways past finding out! . . . For of Him and through Him, and to Him are all things, to whom be glory forever" (Romans 11:33, 36).

GREAT MYSTERIES SOLVED

It is by the Cross, too, that the great mysteries regarding the Lord Jesus Christ, as the Son of Man and the Son of God, are solved; it is at the Cross that so many of the puzzling questions about His person are satisfactorily explained. If man as a sinner under death and judgment is to have one as Savior who can meet his need fully, it requires that that He be a perfect man, as well as perfect God, in order to be a true representative. And so Christ became man, coming into the world as a babe under human conditions, partaking of flesh and blood, that He might destroy him who has the power of death, that is, the devil; and also to make propitiation for the sin of the world. To be a sin-bearer, He must Himself be free from any taint of sin, and that required His being born of a virgin. The virgin birth was an absolute necessity if Jesus Christ was to put away sin by bearing it. If He was not born of a virgin, then He was not sinless, and man has no Savior. If He had come into the world in the ordinary way by human generation, He would have been tainted with sin through Adam, and His death could not then atone for the sin of any other for He would have had to die for His own sin.

Very few cast any doubt upon the fact of the humanity of Christ, for the records of the four evangelists of the gospels describe so forcibly and so fully what a real man He was and how truly human He acted. It is in connection with His deity that so many questions are raised, but these are in the main answered at the Cross; for one of the three witnesses brought forward by John in his first epistle is the blood. "There are three that bear witness on earth: the Spirit, the water, and the blood," he wrote, "and these three agree as one" (1 John 5:8).

The work of redemption was so stupendous that none but God was able to undertake it. Man had so terribly failed, and sin had wrought such awful devastation in the world, that if man was to be redeemed and brought to God and made secure eternally, there must be no possibility of failure in the work. Had that work been entrusted to an angel, there might have been failure; or had any human being been made responsible, however perfect, he might have made some mistake. So in order that the work might be perfect, without any possibility of failure, God Himself undertook it, coming down to earth in the person of His Son. That is what we see at the Cross. "God was in Christ reconciling the world to Himself, not imputing their trespasses to them" (2 Corinthians 5:19).

It was not only the putting away of sin that was necessary, but the bringing of man into fellowship with God and giving him an eternal inheritance, thus providing for him salvation, eternal and perfect. No mere man could have endured the awful sufferings through which the Lord Jesus passed and have borne up under them as He did. "But a body You have prepared for Me" (Hebrews 10:5). In Philippians 2:5–11, which has been used by some to teach the limitations of Christ and to detract from His deity, the words rather witness to deity than mere humanity; for it was only God who could take the place described there and go down to the very death of the cross. That passage really means that Christ so emptied Himself that all He did was in the power of another and done in utter dependence on Him.

That is the very secret of the whole life of the Lord Jesus, including His death on the cross. His every act and word were performed and spoken in the power of God. He could truly say, "The Son can do nothing of

Himself, but what He sees the Father do; for whatever He does, the Son also does in like manner" (John 5:19). On the cross any mere man would have been utterly exhausted by what he had to endure; but on the contrary, when the end came it was with a *loud* voice that He cried, "It is finished!" and then He gave up His spirit. That was the evidence of a divine act.

WHY MAN'S FALL WAS PERMITTED

Why did God allow man to fall into sin? Why was such an awful catastrophe permitted as the fall of man, bringing ruin and misery into the world? Why are men held responsible for their sin, when they are born into the world as sinners? These and many other questions constantly arise in the minds of men, and they are used by many to question the goodness and love of God; and some make them an excuse for their evil ways and their unbelief of the Word of God. These questions are not evidence of special intelligence but rather prove that man is a fallen being and that his mind and thoughts have become corrupted by sin.

The Cross is the one place where sin can be understood and explained. It is there that sin shows itself in all its heinousness and vileness. If we are to judge the awfulness of a crime, we do so by the penalty meted out to the one who commits it. For example, if a man is sentenced to death, we at once infer, and rightly so, that he was guilty of some terrible criminal act. Since, therefore, sin could not be put away except by the awful death suffered by the Son of God on the cross, how terrible that sin must be and how heinous in the sight of God. Or, again, in the case of a disease, the seriousness of the remedy called for indicates the character of the malady; for if a doctor pronounces amputation as necessary where some limb is diseased, we naturally infer that the disease is incurable otherwise. Even so, in the case of sin, there is no pardon or deliverance from it and its effects but by death, and that by the death of the cross. "He made Him who knew no sin to be sin for us, that we might become the righteousness of God in Him" (2 Corinthians 5:21). He bore the penalty, and He provides a perfect remedy.

It is significant that in Hebrew the same word is rendered "sin" and "sin offering" and "punishment for sin," bearing out what has been pointed out above. It is by the sin offering that we learn what sin truly is and by it is shown the awful punishment that it demands. When men and women have been so fully purged from their sins and delivered from their evil nature that they are able to look upon things as God Himself does, they will be enabled to judge correctly the nature of sin—to realize how awful it is as well as recognize that no punishment can be too severe.

WHY THE DEVIL WAS CREATED

One of the great purposes for which Christ took part of flesh and blood was to destroy the one who has the power of death, that is, the devil: "For this purpose the Son of God was manifested, that He might destroy the works of the devil" (1 John 3:8). And in Revelation 12, where the devil is spoken of as "the great dragon . . . that serpent of old, called the Devil and Satan" and is shown to be "the accuser of our brethren," victory over him is assured "by the blood of the Lamb and by the word of their testimony" (vv. 9–11). These and many other Scripture portions assert that there is a personal devil, the adversary of God and of man—God's highest creation. He goes about as a roaring lion, seeking whom he may devour. He is a liar and the father of lies; and he was a murderer from the beginning. He is the tempter who at the very beginning tempted Eve and led her to take the forbidden fruit and so brought about the Fall recorded in Genesis. His enmity has been directed against mankind ever since.

Many stumble over this truth; they question the wisdom of God in creating the devil and in permitting such a being to live and practice his wiles. They seem to overlook the fact that God created him perfect in his ways, a wonderful being marked by wisdom and beauty. It would appear that he was possibly the most wonderful being that God ever created. He was "the anointed cherub who covers" (Ezekiel 28:14) and was evidently given a position of great responsibility in the purposes of God. But through pride he fell from his high estate and became the archenemy of God and of truth. The very causes which brought about his fall were the ones which were used by him to bring about the fall of man. The serpent assured Eve that by taking the fruit of the forbidden tree, she and Adam would become as gods, thus ministering to pride. And instead of being submissive to the will of God, she acted in self-will, which is the very essence of sin, for that is lawlessness.

The Cross of Christ was the culmination of all the malice and enmity of the devil towards God and man; and yet when he doubtless thought that he was achieving a wonderful victory and was putting the Lord Jesus out of the way, he did not realize that the act of Christ in giving Himself a sacrifice for mankind meant his own destruction and final doom. The whole history of sin and evil, having its origin in the devil and his machinations, is therefore explained by the work of Christ on the cross.

ETERNAL PUNISHMENT

The truth above all others which gives rise to criticism and murmuring, even among many professing believers in the Word of God, is that of eternal punishment and hell. We must admit that we can know absolutely nothing about the future life and what lies beyond the grave, except by revelation; so that we are shut up to the Scriptures as the only medium of light. Apart from the Bible, no one knows anything on these great and solemn subjects. But when we turn to the Word of God, we find that the great authority and teacher on these themes is none other than the

Lord Jesus Himself. He spoke with no uncertain sound when He said, "These will go away into everlasting punishment, but the righteous into eternal life" (Matthew 25:46). Three times these very solemn words came from His lips, "Where 'their worm does not die, and the fire is not quenched'" (Mark 9:44, 46, 48).

It is not the intention here to go into the teaching on this subject, except to refer to it in the light of the Cross. If there were no great dangers to sinners and no awful hereafter, the act of God in giving up His Son to such a dreadful death on the cross, and to such terrible sufferings as He there endured, would be criminal. The Cross proves conclusively that there must be an awful future for those who die in their sin, or it would be inconceivable that a holy, wise, and righteous God, who is full of love and compassion, would allow His only Son to be put to such shame under the curse and judgment of God. The shallow view of sin and its awfulness, and the efforts of man to explain away eternal punishment, originate with wrong views of the Cross and man's failure to enter in its meaning as the only atonement for sin and its guilt.

There can be little doubt that very many will have a terrible awakening someday, when the solemn realities of eternity burst upon them; and there will be no question then of the dreadfulness of sin and its awful consequences. Nor will there be any question regarding the justice of God in the punishment of guilty sinners in the awful fires of hell. The solemn words of Isaiah 66:24 will then have their literal fulfillment: "And they shall go forth and look upon the corpses of the men who have transgressed against Me. For their worm does not die, and their fire is not quenched. They shall be an abhorrence to all flesh."

THE JEWISH PERSECUTION

The very sad history of the Jewish nation and the terrible persecutions that have been inflicted upon that people have been a puzzle to many; for is not that nation the chosen one of God and precious in His sight? As already noticed, the purposes of God to plant Israel in their own land and make them a blessing to the other nations of the world must yet be fulfilled as prophesied. There again, it is the Cross that gives light to such prophecies and clears away perplexity. This was wonderfully proved to one great soul among that people, and his experience illustrates what we are contending for with regard to the Cross.

Joseph Rabinowitch was a prominent Jew living in Russia and was greatly concerned about his own people. He sought to do what he could to alleviate their sufferings caused by the persecutions through which they were passing. He joined the Palestine Colonization Movement and went to the Holy Land in order to see what could be done to arrange for transporting many Jews from Russia to their own land. One day in Palestine, he was sitting on the Mount of Olives, looking down upon the city of Jerusalem. He wondered how it was that that sacred place should be in the hands of Gentiles. He was perplexed at its desolation, for he knew something of its history and of God's purpose for His chosen city, where His glory should rest.

Suddenly it dawned upon that him that the cause was the rejection of Jesus Christ and His crucifixion by the Jews. He put his hand into his pocket where he had a Hebrew New Testament, which he had bought with the idea that it might be some sort of a guide to places in the land. Opening it, his eyes lighted on the fifteenth chapter of John, and he read these words, "I am the vine, you are the branches. . . . Without Me you can do nothing" (v. 5). Right there and then he realized that the crucified Christ was his Savior and Messiah.

Almost at once he left Palestine and returned to Russia, where he began to preach the Gospel to his own people, proclaiming the Lord Jesus Christ as their Savior and Messiah. He was greatly used in turning many to the Lord. It was the Cross that explained to him the whole Jewish position and helped him understand how it was that they were suffering and being persecuted so severely.

BITTERNESS SWEETENED BY CALVARY

Those who believe in a rejected Christ and become His followers need not expect that a world which hated Him and crucified Him will mete out to them any better treatment. Just before the Lord Jesus left this world and ascended to the right hand of God, He assured His disciples that "in the world you will have tribulation" (John 16:33). That was the one thing that He promised them in the world, and it has ever been realized in the experiences of His followers.

There are bitter experiences, perplexities, and many problems and difficulties, even in the Christian life. It is easy to enumerate the evils in the world, the injustices and hardships, with instances where the poor suffer and the innocent are wronged; and there are hosts of happenings in the world, day after day, which are beyond the wisdom of man to explain or understand. But if all these grievances and perplexities are brought to the Cross and examined in the light of what took place there, when the holy and blessed Son of God was put in the place of guilt and judgment, and caused to suffer all the indignities and shame poured upon Him, they are understood in a way otherwise impossible. They become steppingstones to a greater blessing and glory.

Many a believer has proved the power of the Cross to sweeten deep sorrow and to comfort him in most trying circumstances. Since God allowed His beloved Son to be despised and rejected, scorned and mocked, and then put to death in the most shameful way and in the greatest agony, what are the Christians' sufferings, even acute, for a little while, in comparison with His suffering on the cross? "For our light affliction, which is but for a moment, is working for us a far more exceeding and eternal weight of glory" (2 Corinthians 4:17).

In the history of the children of Israel, a section of the people led by Korah, Dathan, and Abiram rebelled against Moses and Aaron, aspired to the priesthood, and brought upon themselves the awful judgment of God. God opened the earth, and they were swallowed up. Immediately afterwards, Moses was told to take twelve rods, representing the twelve tribes of Israel, and lay them in the tabernacle overnight. When he returned to the tabernacle in the morning, he found that one of the rods had budded, brought forth blossoms, and yielded almonds. That was Aaron's rod, and by bringing it to life, God bore witness to Aaron as the high priest. By that sign of resurrection, He rebuked the murmurings of the children of Israel.

Even so, by the resurrection of Christ from among the dead, God has proved to men His wisdom, love, and power in giving Jesus to die for sinners. He has shown that sin has been put away, the power of the devil has been annulled, and the grave has been emptied. Because of the finished work of Christ, sin is now inexcusable, unbelief unpardonable, and all murmurings are shameful and unjustifiable. Every enemy of man has been defeated, and God has provided a Savior who is able to save to the uttermost. Eternal salvation is now offered to everyone as a free gift. Have you received this wonderful gift?